The Certifiable™
SALESPERSON

The Certifiable™
SALESPERSON

THE ULTIMATE GUIDE TO HELP ANY SALESPERSON GO CRAZY WITH UNPRECEDENTED SALES!

TOM HOPKINS
LAURA LAAMAN

John Wiley & Sons, Inc.

THE CERTIFIABLE is a trademark of Executive Training Consultants.

Published by John Wiley & Sons, Inc., Hoboken, New Jersey.
Published simultaneously in Canada.

Limit of Liability/Disclaimer of Warranty: While the publisher and author have used their best efforts in preparing this book, they make no representations or warranties with respect to the accuracy or completeness of the contents of this book and specifically disclaim any implied warranties of merchantability or fitness for a particular purpose. No warranty may be created or extended by sales representatives or written sales materials. The advice and strategies contained herein may not be suitable for your situation. You should consult with a professional where appropriate. Neither the publisher nor author shall be liable for any loss of profit or any other commercial damages, including but not limited to special, incidental, consequential, or other damages.

For general information on our other products and services, or technical support, please contact our Customer Care Department within the United States at 800-762-2974, outside the United States at 317-572-3993 or fax 317-572-4002.

Wiley also publishes its books in a variety of electronic formats. Some content that appears in print may not be available in electronic books.

For more information about Wiley products, visit our web site at www. wiley.com.

Library of Congress Cataloging-in-Publication Data:
Laaman, Laura L., 1965-
   The certifiable salesperson : the ultimate guide to help any salesperson go crazy with unprecedented sales! / by Laura Laaman and Tom Hopkins.
      p. cm.
Includes index.
  ISBN 0-471-28913-2 (alk. paper)
  1. Selling. 2. Sales personnel. I Hopkins, Tom. II. Title.
  HF5438.25 .L325 2002
  658.85—dc21   2002013631
Printed in the United States of America

10 9 8 7 6 5 4 3 2 1

Contents

About the Authors

Laura Laaman

Since 1989, Laura Laaman has been WOWing audiences filled with salespeople, managers and customer service representatives with powerful and entertaining presentations. Laura shares the stage with other top speakers including master sales trainer, Tom Hopkins and world-renowned motivational speaker, Zig Ziglar.

Laura's road to sales success started when she was just 16. She quickly went on to break numerous national sales records. Many remain unsurpassed today. Due to Laura's success, several companies studied her strategy and then modeled their training program around her techniques, producing tremendous results.

After proving her techniques were replicable, Laura discovered she possessed a unique gift for teaching others and founded Executive Training Consultants in 1989. Since then, Laura and her staff have helped thousands of companies in the United States and Europe SELL MORE by using the vital techniques she delivers at her training seminars and presentations.

As an award-winning speaker, new salespeople and veterans alike look up to Laura because of her credibility, and powerful, yet approachable manner.

For more information on Laura Laaman's products and services contact Executive Training Consultants at 1-888-SELL-MORE (1-888-735-5667) or visit her Web site: www.lauralaaman.com.

Tom Hopkins

Tom Hopkins is world-renowned as America's No. 1 sales trainer. For more than 30 years, he has helped millions of sales professionals around the world serve more people through proven-effective selling skills. His simple yet persuasive how-to strategies have increased the incomes of salespeople and companies alike many times over.

Tom was not always successful. His first 90 days in sales, he earned only $150. Through self-education and persistence, however, he soon learned that selling—as a skill like any other—could be honed and fine-tuned. He went on to set real estate sales records that still stand today.

His public seminars sell out, and his customized, private programs receive rave reviews. Tom's books have sold in the millions, and hundreds of thousands of people benefit from his recorded audio and video programs every day.

For more information on Tom Hopkin's products and services, contact Tom Hopkins International at 1-800-528-0446 or visit his Web site: www.tomhopkins.com.

A Message from the Authors

Many professions, including accounting, law, and medicine, have a certification program that sets the standard for success within that particular profession. Until now, the sales industry has not had such a widely accepted tool.

Some progressive businesses have developed a certification program within their companies. Unfortunately, many programs focus on product knowledge and fall short of the sales skills needed to excel. Perhaps not having such a generalized program contributes to the reason why sales has not been given the respect granted to other professions. Such guidelines will help each salesperson understand what strategies are necessary to becoming highly successful.

Such a standard can provide an assurance for the consumer that is expected of other licensed professionals, such as certified public accountants (CPAs) and doctors (MDs) and financial planners.

As trainers and speakers, we have spent years watching thousands of salespeople initially struggle and many succeed. *The Certifiable™ Salesperson* is a comprehensive blueprint of the successful strategies and techniques necessary in any challenging marketplace.

As in other professions, it would be impossible to include all of the elements necessary to succeed in one easy-to-read book. We have, however, provided what we hope you agree is a straightforward snapshot of some of the most important elements covered in our certification program.

Although some, if not many, of these concepts might sound familiar—especially to the seasoned veteran—we are confident that all salespeople will benefit from embracing and implementing these important skills.

If you do not already, we hope that you will come to appreciate and respect the sales profession as much as we do. Finally, we hope that this book will inspire you, stay in your memory and in your heart, and make you and your family wealthier—financially and emotionally.

If you are interested in becoming a certified graduate salesperson and/or receiving *continuing education credit*s (CEUs), go to www.TheCertifiableSalesperson.com to learn about seminar schedules.

The Road to Sales

"Ouch!" Steve cried as he spilled coffee on his pajamas while circling classified ads as he looked for a new job. He reassured himself that with his background he would qualify for a substantial position with a sizeable salary.

Interviews

After many telephone conversations and lots of correspondence, he had quite a few interviews lined up. Steve debated between a striped tie and a solid one as he prepared for his first interview. He felt ready.

The employers were pleasant and seemed interested in hiring him. They told Steve that they would get back to him. After a few days, however, Steve hadn't heard back from any of his interviews. A week later, Steve finally received his first phone call from a company he had interviewed with. As Steve confidently listened and prepared to negotiate a favorable salary, he was surprised when the human resources manager told Steve that he wouldn't be offered the position he had interviewed for. "But we would like to offer you a sales position with our company," she said.

"Sales?" he asked, stunned.

"You're enthusiastic, you seem driven, and your personality seems to be just what we need," she said.

Steve had considered sales in the past. He was initially flattered, but then he learned that although the position came with a significant commission program, the salary was significantly lower than what he was hoping to earn. He politely told the *human resources* (HR) manager that he would have to think it over. Days went by, and there were no additional interview requests. This was getting serious. No money was coming in. He thought, "If something doesn't break soon, I might have to take the sales job."

A week went by, and still no word from any of his other job interviews. "These bills are driving me crazy! I've got to do *something* to earn money." With some reluctance, he called and accepted the position in sales. Steve would be starting in just a few days.

The First Day

Nervous, Steve entered the company's building and met with the receptionist who seemed to be expecting him. Steve's new boss, Mr. Proffett, came out, glanced down at his watch and greeted Steve warmly, thanking him for being on time.

Mr. Proffett led Steve into the training room and introduced Steve to their top salesperson and coach, Tom, who helped with training new salespeople, and seemed genuinely pleased to meet him. There were just a few others in the training room.

Orientation/Training

A rather young woman walked in appearing confident and in charge. She organized her materials, and as she personally greeted everyone, handed each salesperson a workbook and a sales journal.

"Good morning, everyone. My name is Mrs. Sellmore. I'll be your instructor today. I'm excited to welcome all of you to our company."

Suddenly, a man rushed into the conference room appearing very disheveled. He introduced himself as Jack, a new salesperson, and apologized for being late, explaining that he tried a short cut and got lost.

Mr. Proffett was not pleased with Jack's tardiness. Mrs. Sellmore handed materials to Jack, and continued. "Allow me to give you the name of this course." She wrote **"The Certifiable Salesperson"** on the board. "You, like so many other salespeople, probably feel 'certifiable' at this point in time, meaning you feel like you are going crazy without the specific selling skills you need to succeed in sales. Once you've successfully completed the course, you will move from being 'Certifiable' to 'Certified'!

The latecomer, Jack, chuckled, leaned over to Steve and said, "Yeah, certifiable all right. I must be certifiable to even be here." Jack stopped as Mrs. Sellmore glanced at him. She continued and handed each attendee the following evaluation.

"Please complete this questionnaire."

- Do you have a self-imposed, quantified, monthly goal? If so, what is it?

- Please define sales.

- What role or impact do you feel your sales position will play in our company's and country's economy?

- Which mind-expanding exercises do you regularly do, to help you excel in sales?

- What role do you feel your body will play in maximizing your performance in sales?

- What things do you do to care for your body?

- Please explain how visualization will improve your sales.

- What self-analyzing strategies do you use to improve your sales?

- When with a customer, what percentage of your time should be spent discussing the product?

- What adjective would you use to describe an ideal presentation pace?

- How many objections are you prepared to successfully address? Which ones?

- What techniques have you mastered to overcome objections?

- Please list the sales books you have read to date.

Steve wasn't sure what some of the questions meant since he was new to sales, but did his best. Mrs. Sellmore collected the questionnaires and looked over the answers.

Sales Defined

"Like many of you, most people define sales simply as the ability to promote a product. If it were that easy, everyone would be successful in sales."

Mrs. Sellmore clicked her pointer as she spoke, bringing up the first screen of her presentation. "Sales is a complex discipline that consists of being able to:

- Find a product that you truly believe will benefit other people

- Be clear on what that product can do for someone

- Develop the skills to get a customer to focus on the challenge your product or service resolves, and then motivate that customer to improve his or her life with your product or service in a way that outweighs the investment for your product, and…

- Do all of that ethically.

"It sounds simple in concept, but can be challenging in practice. Sales is a profession that is mentally and emotionally demanding. It incorporates always being mentally alert, focused, and able to overcome rejection, working hard, and performing ethically.

When you do this and succeed, you will play an important role in our economy. We can produce and distribute the best product but without great salespeople, our company will fail.

If you can demonstrate that you have the attitude and skills necessary to successfully promote our company and product, you will become a Certified Salesperson."

Why Certified?

"Many other industries, including the medical profession, legal profession, and the world of finance have certification standards that indicate to the company and the customer that an individual has the necessary skills to excel in his or her chosen field."

The sales profession shouldn't be different. We have proven there is a set of behaviors, specific guidelines, and skills necessary to excel in sales. Mrs. Sellmore encouraged the attendees to take many notes in the sales journals she had provided them. She explained taking notes is an important skill used by the top salespeople within her company, as well as other industries. She appreciated the initiative of a few who brought legal pads, but encouraged them to place their notes in the sales journal as it would be the place they would look back to for all their new strategies, as well as, to track their future successes. Steve did so. Mrs. Sellmore gave an exciting presentation about the history of the company, its merchandise, and its superb customer satisfaction rate.

"Our company is growing and we need enthusiastic, dedicated, career-minded salespeople to help spread the message about our great products and services to prospective customers.

Each of you, during this training period, will be exposed to the same proven lessons, necessary to excel in sales. Out of this group, just like most groups, there will most likely be three levels of success. A few will take this career seriously and do very well financially. The second group *could* do just as well, but won't work hard enough, and, consequently, will only do marginally well. The last group of people will discover that selling isn't for them for one reason or another. Obviously, that group won't be with us very long."

Steve liked the 'very well financially' part of what Mrs. Sellmore said. He couldn't help but ask her, "Could you clarify what 'very well financially' means?"

As if she were prepared for the question, she clicked her pointer and the next screen came up. The screen showed the sales staff's sales volume numbers and commissions year-to-date. A man named Tom was making more money than Steve imagined a top executive could make. "How could someone *in sales* make *that* much money?" he asked himself. Steve wondered if this was the same Tom he had been introduced to.

Steve leaned forward in his chair and listened as attentively as he could. The training continued for the rest of the day and ended with Mrs. Sellmore assigning homework. She encouraged everyone to write down the homework assignment in their new sales journals. So Steve did.

Steve worked on his homework that evening. He was pleasantly surprised how interesting he found it.

The next day, before class started, his other classmates introduced themselves. Among them were Wendy and Jack. Wendy was pleasant, seemed eager, but had a little sales experience. Jack boasted about his extensive sales background. Steve was surprised that Jack was in this training session at all. Steve thought Jack could be a lot of help during this session, so he moved his things and sat next to him.

Mrs. Sellmore entered and enthusiastically started with a brief summary of the previous day's material. After the quick review, she asked everyone to take out their homework.

Jack leaned over to Steve and said, "I can't believe anyone would do that stupid homework; I certainly didn't."

Mrs. Sellmore went around the room asking everyone to explain to the rest of the group what they learned from their homework. She began with Wendy. Wendy did the homework, but complained that it was very difficult and took a great deal of time.

Mrs. Sellmore called on Jack next. Amazingly, he had a credible and valid excuse as to why he had not completed his homework, one he conveniently forgot to mention to Steve moments before.

"I see," Mrs. Sellmore said. "Sales, like any other career, is going to give you back exactly what you put into it. I hope this is just a glitch in your path to success.

"Let's move on. What do you think of when you imagine what a great salesperson is like?"

Answers included some typical, negative responses: poor quality or ill-fitting clothes, someone who is so pushy that you hope he or she doesn't corner you at a party, and loud-mouthed.

"In contrast, let's study the traits and develop the skills of top-producing, great salespeople.

Lesson 1—The Mind and Body of a Great Salesperson

Attitude

Mrs. Sellmore continued. "The following lessons may appear simple to even a seasoned salesperson. We have discovered that unsuccessful or average salespeople, however, have not taken the time to fully understand, implement, and master these lessons. Great salespeople have. The payoff of this commitment will be high productivity and profitability.

Over the years, we have found that there are two ways to work through this material. The first is with the attitude of 'I've heard that before' and, therefore, dismiss the material. The second way is with this attitude: 'I've heard that before but I have not yet implemented it' or 'I'm not doing that as well as I could.'

The most important trait of a top salesperson is having a highly optimistic attitude. The profession of sales is filled with ups and downs. Accepting this, the disciplined salesperson incorporates numerous strategies to stay optimistic."

Attitude Food

"There are countless wonderful, inspirational messages with which you can feed your spirit. These can be as simple as quotes or as involved as personal stories by people who have every reason to not be happy, yet remain so. In fact, there are inspirational services that can be sent to you via e-mail daily, free of charge. Others can be found in books and sometimes in the newspaper.

It's hard to get too upset about the little things when you learn how someone who has every good reason to be negative (including being gravely ill or a person who just lost someone close to him or her) isn't. When you surround yourself with inspiration, it is easier to move on and get back to work when things don't go well."

Visualization

"When a great salesperson gets out of bed, he assumes it will be a great day. Why does he think that? Maybe his mind and body are biased that way, or maybe his brain and psyche have figured out that if he believes that, it probably will happen. Does it? More often than not, yes. When you be-lieve something, that belief will influence the outcome. Unfortunately, in every profession things don't always go according to plan, and negative things sometimes do happen. Great performers know they have to get their minds on the best track possible and use a technique called positive visualization."

Positive visualization has roots in imagery.[1] Imagery is an extremely effective strategy that facilitates making changes in our lives. Imagery is a biological process that people use every day without being aware of it. One of the differences between humans and other animals is our ability to incorporate imagery into our subconscious minds.

Studies have shown that the average person has about 10,000 random thoughts each day. Sadly, about 50 percent of those thoughts are negative. Salespeople will not be successful if they view their futures negatively. Potential clients can sense whether or not you believe in your product, and that will influence a positive or negative outcome. In fact, we consistently have found that people will make purchasing decisions based more on your conviction and enthusiasm than they will on your product knowledge.

Programmed visualization is a process by which we consciously control the images going into our minds by 'talking' to our subconscious. Successful athletes often use this type of imagery to improve performance and for healing, positive reinforcement, and achieving goals. So, whether your goal is a marathon or a particular sale, visualization can help you get there.

By devoting just five minutes to conscious, positive visualization three times each day, we can erase hours, days, or weeks of negative thoughts. Just as our bodies need constant nutrition in the form of healthy meals each day, our minds also need to be nourished. Regular, positive visualization can quickly eliminate old habits, attitudes, and thinking patterns a person has had for years.[2]

World-class high jumpers visualize themselves clearing the bar even before they can. Professional football players imagine themselves winning the Super Bowl; great salespeople will benefit from taking the time to imagine themselves being successful in sales.

Guarding Your Attitude Jealously

Great salespeople guard their attitudes jealously and do not hang around negative people. They understand doing so would deplete their positive energy and productivity. It's difficult to maintain your enthusiasm when others around you are dismal and depressed. Enthusiasm is contagious, however. If you can hang on to a positive attitude despite any negativity around you, you likely will inspire others to become enthusiastic.

Ask yourself right now: How would you describe your attitude overall? Are you always optimistic, generally optimistic, sometimes optimistic, or not usually optimistic?

Here is a simple example of programming. Each morning when you get up and rush out of bed to the alarm clock, ask—or better yet, tell yourself—what kind of day you are going to have. Your mind and spirit will help make it happen. This visualization is paramount in sales. When you feel positive, your customers are far more likely to want to do business with you.

Looking at and Dealing with Change

Now, ask yourselves how well you think you deal with change.

Steve realized that change was a big deal in some industries, including the medical profession and the scientific field. Yet, he had to really think about how change could impact a salesperson.

Mrs. Sellmore continued, "Products change, customers change, competition changes, sales presentations and economies change. Great salespeople understand the importance of having proper attitudes and skills to stay with—or better, ahead of—all those changes."

Steve thought about how his life had changed recently. He was in a new job with a new company. He was learning things that he had never thought about before. He was being optimistic that this change was for the good. Time would tell.

Jack whispered, "Things change all right; the last company I worked for went out of business."

Mrs. Sellmore continued, "Change is a part of life. Not only will the market and economy change, but also, hopefully, so will a particular product and company change—for the better. The more progressive companies look ahead and either stay with, or better—ahead of change. These companies will make a lot of good moves and sometimes may suffer temporary setbacks. Either way, they don't need or want to have a negative staff member—especially a salesperson fighting change."

The Body of a Great Salesperson

"Top salespeople work as hard on themselves as on their careers. They treat their bodies like the multi-million-dollar machines that they are and take care of them with the same reverence that athletes have for their bodies.

Salespeople must handle a lot of stress-related issues, such as customer moods, rejection, management pressures, quotas, changes in economy, budgets. ... Yet, most salespeople do not take positive steps to deal with this stress. They operate reactively to stress rather than proactively.

United States Presidents face enormous stress on a daily basis. Presidents Clinton and George W. Bush found that jogging reduced stress and helped them create new energy and productivity. Many of our top salespeople exercise in the morning before work. They feel that it helps them better prepare for their days. Exercise provides both physical and emotional rewards. Exercise can lower your blood pressure, lower your total blood cholesterol, and stabilize your blood sugar. These physical effects decrease the risk of stroke, heart disease, and diabetes.[3]

Exercise also affects brain chemistry and provides many emotional benefits, including an improved sense of wellbeing, increased emotional stamina, and improved sleep.

Other types of exercise, such as weight-lifting and stretching, can improve muscle strength, bone density, and flexibility. Such exercise improves endurance, dexterity, and balance.

After you check with your physician, and you commit to 30–40 minutes of exercise a day, five days a week, the return on your investment will be enormous—physically, mentally, emotionally, and financially.[4] If you are just starting out, please don't be overwhelmed. When I first started exercising, I couldn't jog down the block. If you have been a couch potato for some time, committing to parking at the far end of the parking lot or taking the stairs instead of the elevator is a good place to start. Walking is terrific for you! A brisk, two-mile walk should not take more than 30–40 minutes of your day.

Extra Fuel for Your Body—Vitamins, Minerals, and Water...

"Many studies have shown that people who take vitamin and mineral supplements regularly, along with eating wellbalanced meals, feel better, are not sick as often, can withstand stress more effectively, and are generally in better health than those who do not follow this path.

Top salespeople typically bring fresh fruits and vegetables to work. They seem convinced that this activity, along with a few other improvements, contributes to their high sales and increased income.[5] Consider your current diet, and begin today with small changes—adding more fruits and vegetables and cutting back on carbohydrates, replacing caffeine with water, and minimizing sweets.

Water plays an important part in keeping your body hydrated and healthy. Drinking a proper amount of quality water helps remove toxins from your body.

Massage

"Medical research has shown that when our muscles and skin are massaged, the circulation increases in our bodies. When that happens, more oxygen and nutrients reach all parts of our bodies more effectively.[6] Including an occasional massage into your health habits can help your overall sense of well-being."

Sleep

"Salespeople are notorious for pushing life to its limit, including their bodies. Research has shown, however, that 63 percent of Americans in general do not get the suggested eight hours of sleep that they need. These studies also show that 51 percent of the American population is so tired that they sometimes have a difficult time doing their jobs during the day.

Just as in other disciplines and sports, to be successful in sales you should be in top shape physically and mentally. If you get eight hours of sleep regularly and take time to exercise, preferably before you start your work schedule, you will be well on your way to becoming more effective in sales and healthier in general.[7]

Now, on to your problem-solving abilities."

Problem-Solving Exercises

"Great salespeople are great problem solvers. Studies have shown that people who regularly expand their vocabularies by reading, and taking part in other mentally-demanding activities, such as completing crossword puzzles, playing chess, and games like Scrabble™, are more effective in problem-solving situations at work.[8]

Listening to classical music helps expand the mind as well. Although it might not be your first music choice, studies have shown that classical music stimulates a part of the brain that increases healing and learning.

Doing all of these things might initially seem unrelated to doing a great job with closing more sales. We are confident, however, that after you make these practices part of your routine, you will experience the same positive results as our top performers."

Lesson 2—Discipline of a Top Salesperson

Countless salespeople get into sales because they are looking for an easy job. Sales looks like a job to which you can report later than, let's say, a factory worker; wear nicer clothes; not get as dirty; not have to perform as much manual labor; and put in fewer hours. Depending on the product you market, most of those are simply myths. While sales must be conducted during hours convenient to clients and might involve starting later than your typical factory worker, there is a great deal of preparation that should take place prior to and after each client contact. You must also dress appropriately for sales, which can include wearing nice clothes. Although manual labor might be at a minimum, mental labor is at an all-time high for the professional salesperson.

Do the More Difficult Task First

Top salespeople make a commitment to do the more difficult task first, even when it's uncomfortable. This action will normally be the most productive use of your time. Rather than having a difficult task hanging over your head all day, you'll get it out of the way early and not let it be a drain on your energy.

Ask yourself what you think the most difficult part of sales will be for you. There's bound to be some aspect of selling that you are not very excited about. Many salespeople do not like prospecting, closing, or asking for referrals. They like the results those activities bring, but are often uncomfortable doing them at first. We will cover powerful strategies on each of these topics shortly. First, *you* need to decide how much you are going to apply yourself.

This strategy is another huge competitive advantage—figuring out the potentially most rewarding tasks, which are often the most difficult and most avoided by others, and doing them. Great salespeople, like great athletes, don't let discomfort stop them. They know that often the more difficult tasks end up producing the greatest rewards.

A great salesperson does his homework. He gets up early and prepares for his day, filling his mind with education and motivation that will benefit him, his company, and most importantly—his customer. He invests the time to research his customer's business, changes in the business climate, and competing companies. Sometimes this process can be done well in just eight hours a day. Other times, you might have to consider this part of your job as homework. One of the goals of this training is to help you work as effectively as possible to keep both your career and your personal life balanced and fulfilled.

Preparation Prior to an Appointment

Salespeople who meet a potential client and haven't done their homework have a serious strike against them. In contrast, the prepared salesperson has a strong competitive advantage. People are very impressed with the strong work ethic demonstrated by a high level of preparation.

In business-to-business sales, there is a wealth of knowledge accessible to you about your prospective customer's industry, company, and maybe even something about him or her personally. In retail or business-to-consumer sales, you should rely on demographic information that's available about your best potential customers.

Here is some foundational homework that you should do before any business appointment:

- **Visit the business's Web site.** The "About Us" page should give you valuable information about the company's history, including founders and other decision-makers. For the proper pronunciation of names, call the company and ask the receptionist.

- **Do a search on the company.** You might find past articles, press releases, and other timely, valuable information.

- **Do a search on the industry.** Industry magazines will probably pop up. They may give you a great deal of timely information, including challenges facing your prospective customer that your product or service will solve.

- **Do a search on the individual with whom you are meeting.** You might find out that he or she is active in a group or charity. You could also learn of other accomplishments that show common interests you share with him or her.

- **Get copies of the company's product brochures and/or catalogs.** Talk with one of its customer service representatives about what the company offers.

- **Always be on time.** Being late personally offends many people. Take all of the steps necessary to arrive five minutes early, including having directions and a plan for detours.

Reading

Sadly, most salespeople have not completely read one sales book or attended one sales training seminar. Can you imagine a specialist in medicine who doesn't attend conferences to learn about the changes in research or the newest breakthrough in technology?

Most people within the sales industry and nearly all those outside of the profession do not realize that these are necessary steps that must be taken in order to be an effective and professional salesperson. This is one reason why there's such a discrepancy between great salespeople and others who struggle within the sales industry.

Great salespeople read continually. They read every sales book they can get their hands on, listen to tapes or CDs in the car, and read industry and professional magazines. In addition to sales and industry books and magazines, we also encourage you to read about philosophy. Reading these types of works, in particular Plato and Socrates, will help inspire your deductive and problem-solving ability. These skills will help you find great solutions to your customer's situations.

Lesson 3—The Likeability of a Great Salesperson

Great salespeople are well-liked. Great salespeople are positive, amiable people and a pleasure to be around. One of the most visible characteristics that makes these people delightful is their enthusiasm. Great salespeople also know how to make others feel important, which makes them likeable to others.

Enthusiasm

"People are drawn to enthusiastic people and businesses like magnets," Mrs. Sellmore said. "For example, one of the most common questions people ask each other in both professional and personal situations is, 'How are you?' whether they've met for the first time or they've known each other for years."

"Wendy, how are you?" Mrs. Sellmore asked.

"I'm fine?" Wendy said, wondering why Mrs. Sellmore would ask such a question now in the middle of the training presentation.

"Jack," Mrs. Sellmore said, "How are you?"

"I'm OK," Jack mumbled.

"Class," continued Mrs. Sellmore, "ask yourselves on a scale of one to 10, one being low, and 10 being high, how enthusiastic the responses 'fine' or 'OK' are. Although they are both common answers, when you're trying to make a connection with someone, 'fine' or 'OK' won't get you very far."

Ask yourselves why most people answer with 'fine' or 'OK.' I believe it's a habit they grew up with, and they choose those words to not draw attention to themselves or stand out.

Great salespeople *should* stand out in a positive, enthusiastic way. Better responses when asked the question, "How are you?" include: "I'm great! How are you?", "I'm terrific! How are you?", "I'm excellent! How are you?", or "I'm unbelievable!" That one covers your situation whether it is good or bad. Choose the best response for you, and deliver it with enthusiasm.

When the first impression you create is enthusiastic, you're off to an excellent start, and you will positively capture someone's attention. This strategy is an easy competitive advantage and has been known to improve one's outlook on life.

Steve and Wendy listened, intrigued. Jack sulked and sat slumped in his chair. He appeared to think the whole exercise was stupid.

Mrs. Sellmore recognized Jack's negative body language but continued. "Starting off on an enthusiastic note is critical to making a connection."

Wendy raised her hand and said, "What if we don't feel great? Are you suggesting we should still say we are?"

"If you've done all of the things we've discussed so far to take care of yourself and prepare for your business day, you should be able to sincerely answer in the positive!" Mrs. Sellmore explained. "These responses will also act as a prompt for you to be 'great,' to be more positive, to appreciate all the positive aspects of the world, and be more enthusiastic! No one wants to spend time with someone who is negative or unenthusiastic. You want your clients to look forward to seeing you, to remember you as being someone positive to be around and someone who makes them feel good."

"Isn't that phony?" Wendy asked.

"No. It's the image you want to illustrate as a sales professional. If you like what you do, it should be easy to adopt a positive attitude when going into a selling situation. Mrs. Sellmore added. "It may not be easy to adapt to this new approach in the beginning. However, top salespeople are willing to shed old habits and replace them with better ones."

One of the best compliments you can receive is when someone asks you why you are 'great,' 'terrific', 'excellent,' or 'unbelievable.' That means they heard you, and you piqued their interest.

Great responses include:

"It's **great** to be here today!"

"I'm **pleased** to meet with you today!"

"Business is **excellent!**"

"I **enjoy** what I do."

"It's an **extraordinary** day."

"I **truly enjoy** helping people like you and companies like yours."

Steve chuckled as he remembered a sales clerk's answer a few days earlier when he asked her how she was. She responded with, "Better in 10 minutes. That's when I'm outta here."

"Being exciting is a key to being well-liked," Mrs. Sellmore said.

"What do you mean by 'exciting?'" Steve asked.

Many Ways to Be More Exciting

Being exciting goes far beyond the use of exciting words. People 'listen' to our actions far more than our words. We process information that we hear at at a far greater rate than someone speaks. In other words, we are able to hear a lot more than just someone's words. By examining your communication style—words and body language—thoroughly, you will uncover numerous opportunities to create a more dynamic connection with those around you, and that will help you sell more.

Albert Mehrabian conducted a now-famous study on how people interpret what you are telling them. According to Mehrabian, people interpret messages by using three modes of communication: verbal, vocal, and visual. (For more on this topic, see his book, *Silent Messages*.)[9] The following chart illustrates how much of each mode can be attributed to the total message.

Mode of Communication	Percent of Message
Verbal (words)	7%
Vocal (tone, pitch, and so on)	38%
Visual (body language)	55%

If you doubt the impact that body language has on us all, think about past Presidential debates and elections. Negative gestures have haunted numerous ex-Presidential candidates.

A successful command of positive body language has helped elect current and past Presidents.

Make Your Nonverbal Messages Exciting: Gestures

Starting with the visual, here are five top positive body language gestures to make yourself more exciting, more attractive, and therefore more successful in sales:

1.   Smiling

Smiling is one of the most effective nonverbal gestures you can employ to create a positive image. If you want to be a top professional and make more money, smile more. Smile when you are listening and even speaking. Not an ear-to-ear fake smile but rather a sincere 'I'm interested and enjoy what I do' smile.

2.   Eye contact

When you make eye contact with an individual, you are saying, "I am interested; I want to, and I can help." Most salespeople do not make enough eye contact. They are focused on other things, including their product or paperwork—more than their customer. The combination of smiling and eye contact is very positive and powerful.

3. Nodding

When someone is speaking, it might not be possible to verbally confirm and assure them that you are listening and understanding. Head nodding is an important non-verbal gesture that can do both. When *you* yourself are speaking, nodding your head will promote agreement and help open the listener up to your point of view.

4. Lean forward

When sitting, use your own back to sit up straight, not the back of the chair. This effort demonstrates your enthusiasm, work ethic, and interest in your customer. If you lean back often, you might be perceived as a lazy or uninterested businessperson who is just going through the motions.

Steve thought about his own gestures and wondered whether he would be perceived as sloppy because he often slouched. Steve glanced over at Jack. He was resting his head on his hand—almost as if he were falling asleep. Wendy appeared attentive, was taking notes, but had her feet propped up on another desk. Steve sat up straight and listened carefully.

5. Open-handed gestures

Open-handed gestures reflect honesty and will increase your credibility. The open hand, particularly the open palm, is still

used for such solemn ceremonies as swearing-in in a court-
room. You will immediately increase the power of your connection with people by making a conscious effort to use
open-hand gestures when you communicate.

Gestures to Avoid

Just as positive body language sends positive messages, negative body language sends negative ones. Be aware of your
own posture and stance at all times. Here are three of the
biggest body language errors that most salespeople make:

1.   Folded arms

Even though you may just be cold, folding your arms across
your chest can communicate to others that you are closed or
defensive.

"This is wasting my time," Jack said under his breath to
Wendy as he crossed his arms and sank deeper into his chair.

"You may cross your arms because you are cold, but the message you are sending is still one of negativity," Mrs. Sellmore
continued. "Wear warmer clothing, including long underwear,
if necessary. Do whatever it takes to free up your arms and
hands so you can use them to express positive gestures."

2.   Hands in pockets

"Hands in the pockets are often interpreted as a sign of inse-
curity or suspicious behavior," Mrs. Sellmore said. "When
your hands are in your pockets, they are not open and visible.
Additionally, you probably have to slouch while your hands

are in your pockets. Worse still is jingling the change in your pocket. It's a distraction."

Jack snickered out loud as if the material was beneath him. Wendy still sat with her arms crossed.

3.   Hiding behind barriers

Wendy asked whether standing behind a counter was negative.

"How did you feel when someone, let's say a teacher or principal, sat behind a big desk?" Mrs. Sellmore asked.

"Intimidated," Wendy replied.

"Exactly," said Mrs. Sellmore. "When you are working on making a connection with someone, if possible come out from behind the counter or desk. Sit or stand next to the individual, almost face to face, but slightly offset (depending whether the other person is sitting or standing)."

Other gestures or nonverbal postures to avoid include turning your back on a person, touching or rubbing your neck (it communicates frustration), and pointing (it is rude and uses closed hands). If you must point something out, use a pointer or a pen or gesture with your whole, open hand rather than your pointer finger. Looking at someone over your glasses can be interpreted as demeaning, and rubbing your hands together suggests greediness.

"When you begin making changes and using positive body language, it may feel staged and even phony," Mrs. Sellmore said. "That is not its intent. Countless salespeople everyday who truly want the best for their customers inadvertently use body language that turns their customers off. Our intention here is to help eliminate those mixed, or even negative messages."

Great salespeople understand the impact body language has on how people perceive them emotionally. Although customers might not have been professionally trained in body language, they will interpret your mood, confidence, and trustworthiness through your body and facial gestures instinctually. This overall impression will dictate whether they trust and like you. If they don't like you or trust you, they probably won't buy from you and you won't be successful in sales.

Genuineness and Sincerity

As important as it is to be exciting, it is even more important to balance that excitement with a sincere understanding and caring for the people you serve. The human being is a very intuitive creature and can tell whether you are merely interested in a quick sale or if you care about finding a solution to the problem. They can see it in your body and hear it in your voice.

At the break, Steve commented to the other students how much sense the information made. He felt he would now have better insight that would help him assist his potential clients. The same information, he hoped, would allow him to be accepted and liked by his clients and coworkers.

Jack chimed in with, "People like me just fine. I can't imagine how all of this is going to help me sell more. I have no plans to work on the way I sit, the way I move, what I say when people ask me how I'm doing and all the rest of this stuff. It's what I tell them that makes the difference in whether or not I sell them."

Lesson 4 —The Voice of a Great Salesperson

Shortly, we will give you the best strategies and words to gain a tremendous amount of business. Please realize everyday however, salespeople say 'the right words' but say them in the 'wrong way' because they haven't honed their voices for the 'right delivery'.

Your voice says a lot about you. It tells people whether you are excited about what you're doing, whether you are confident, and whether you care. If you are not excited about what you sell or the company you're selling for, your customers probably will not be either, and they will go somewhere else. People buy more on your belief and conviction than on your product knowledge. That's why it is so important to sell a product you truly believe in, and if feasible, that you use yourself.

Your voice includes your pitch, tone, enunciation, and inflection. A word spoken in an upbeat, enthusiastic tone will sound different than the same word spoken in a monotone voice.

One example is the word "Hello." Depending on your tone, it will translate as, "Hi! I am thrilled to meet you," or "Hello. I really wish I were somewhere else."

Your voice also tells a customer whether you expect him or her to buy. Most customers are looking for their sales professionals to take the lead. Your voice represents your level of confidence. Most salespeople have never thought about how important their voices are in helping them become successful in sales.

Mrs. Sellmore clicked to the next screen:

All I need is your approval and we're all set

"Is this a question or a statement?" Mrs. Sellmore asked.

The group didn't know because there was no punctuation.

"When punctuation isn't visible as with the spoken word, your voice makes the punctuation for you—and your customer," Mrs. Sellmore said.

She went around the room and asked each attendee to say the words on the screen and asked the group to listen to the way each person's voice ended in relation to the way it began—either higher or lower.

Steve noticed that some of the attendees made their statements sound like questions. Others sounded like statements—more confident.

Mrs. Sellmore saw that Jack again appeared visibly bored. She tried to involve him and asked him how the control of his voice would impact his success in sales.

"I have *no idea*," Jack responded in an extremely uninterested tone.

"Two salespeople can make the same presentation and both ask for the customer's business using the exact same words. If one ends the closing statement with the voice moving in an upward tone on the word 'set,' it sounds like a question," she said.

An elevation in your tone of voice at the end of your closing statement will tell the customer that you are unsure whether your closing statement worked. If the other salesperson ends the statement with the voice in a descending tone, as if making a declaration, then—all things being equal—the latter is more likely to get the sale. A slight downward tone at the end will tell your customer that you are confident in your statement, and you assume that the purchase will happen.

"People want to work with and take advice from a professional who sounds confident," Mrs. Sellmore said. Practicing, recording and critiquing your voice inflection will help you improve your voice and sales."So, *now* can we get to the sales pitch?" Jack asked impatiently.

"I'm glad you brought that up," replied Mrs. Sellmore.

Lesson 5—The Image of a Great Salesperson

"Now that we've looked on the inside, let's talk about what a customer sees, hears, and feels while he's with you," Mrs. Sellmore said as she clicked to the next screen.

"This may seem basic to you, but it's critical to understand," she continued. "Every day sales are lost, not because the salesperson didn't care about her customer or possessed a lack of product knowledge, but because of the image they presented."

Clothing

Today's business dress has become more relaxed than it was just a few short years ago; some would say that this shift parallels the decline in many people's work ethics. The trend of relaxed dress has created an easy, competitive edge for smart salespeople.

If you question whether higher standards will make a difference, create a test for your situation. Adopt a more polished and conservative dress for one month. You will undoubtedly find that when you are conservatively dressed and polished, customers, supervisors, and maybe even a few coworkers will treat you with more respect and be more receptive to your services and ideas.

Steve remembered going into a computer store wearing a business suit and noticing the high level of attention that he received.

Mrs. Sellmore continued, "You probably have gone into a store dressed in a suit and had another customer approach you to ask whether you worked there. You looked as if you were someone in authority. We judge people when we first meet them—often in the first 30 seconds or less. Much of this judgment is based on what those people are wearing and how well they're groomed."

Steve remembered a friend, a small business CEO, who often excused himself from interviews to view applicants' cars. He believed that the inside of a car was an indicator of the quality of their work and work ethic—and that a messy car meant messy work.

Mrs. Sellmore continued, "Top salespeople know that their images need to represent trust. People are more likely to trust and treat you as an authority figure if you are conservatively dressed.[10] Look at trusted people we all know: Dan Rather, Tom Brokaw, Oprah Winfrey, and Barbara Walters."

Attention to detail is crucial to your prospective customer as well as to your supervisors. You can register this trust subconsciously or consciously. Here are some tips.

Successful Image Hints for Men and Women

- Business suit coats and/or blazers demonstrate authority and increase credibility. The cut should be a current style or at least not out of date, otherwise out of date is the impression that will be made.

- Excellent grooming (including hands and teeth) clean and polished, conservative dress shoes demonstrate an attention to detail.

- A clean, conservative hairstyle promotes trust.

- A light fragrance is fine, but too much perfume or cologne can be a real turn-off.

- Minimal jewelry, including no visible body piercing beyond conservative, pierced earrings for women

- No gum, candy, or other objects in your mouth

- A confident handshake

It was time for the group to take a break. Jack came over to Steve and slapped him on the back. "So what do you think about all this? Pretty lame, huh?" he said.

Without giving Steve a chance to respond, Jack looked down at his shoes that were in need of a good shine and said, "If this place pays me good enough, I'll be the first one to run out and get me some good clothes."

Steve noticed Jack's poor grammar and someone's horrible cologne. He wasn't sure if it was Jack's or Wendy's, but he decided to excuse himself and get a bottle of water. After the break, they all returned to their seats.

What Your Handshake Says About You

Mrs. Sellmore resumed her discussion. "Your handshake speaks volumes about who you are—your level of confidence and your energy level," she said. "Make sure your handshake says what you want it to say. A firm, but not overpowering, handshake helps you to more effectively connect with others, including your prospective customer. Bend your elbow a bit when you offer your hand to help decrease the distance between you and your customer. When you start your handshake, direct your palm slightly upward. This body language suggests openness and trustworthiness."

Whether you are a man or a woman, remember to shake hands with everyone in the group, starting with the person who is nearest to you and then shake everyone else's hand while making direct eye contact and smiling. If you do not know the name of someone in the group and that person hasn't been introduced to you, shake that person's hand, introduce yourself, and ask his or her name.

Now, ask yourself, "How will I improve my image?" Specifically, what can you improve with regard to your clothing, your hair, your jewelry, your shoes, and your handshake?

Lesson 6—The Need for and Art of Friendly Control

"Now that we know how to look the part of a top professional, let's discuss how to communicate like one," Mrs. Sellmore said.

Another major difference between successful salespeople and unsuccessful salespeople is that successful salespeople take friendly control. People appreciate being guided, not pushed, when they require new knowledge in order to make a wise decision.

Great salespeople realize that their prospective clients might not have purchased this type of product before, and even if they have, then probably not this exact model and not from them or their company. This inexperience might leave the customer uncertain about what to do or say or in what order. This discomfort works against a positive outcome.

Great salespeople are willing and able to use friendly control to guide the customer throughout the transaction.

"I'm confident you will agree that accountants, teachers, and doctors need to take 'friendly control' in their chosen professions," Mrs. Sellmore said. "Doctors, in order to ensure a healthy, healed patient, need to understand what is going on with that patient. A patient may come into a doctor's office and quickly expect a particular prescription. A good doctor works to avoid misdiagnosis by taking friendly control and moving through the standard process of diagnosis and treatment. The conscientious doctor avoids any short cuts that might result in a misdiagnosis or mistreatment."

Sales is no different. Great salespeople want to understand what is wrong or what can be improved in a potential client's life. They need to determine how they can make the situation better for the customer. To perform this task, a great salesperson takes *friendly* control. In contrast, if a salesperson lets a customer say simply what she believes she needs, without the salesperson following the proper steps, there will not be the necessary rapport, no appreciation of the company and product, and probably no sale.

"Simple ways of taking friendly control are by using assumptive actions and words," Mrs. Sellmore explained.

Assumptive Words

Assumptive words can help you engage and lead a prospective customer from the moment of first contact, even if it's over the phone. Even though a caller may not have asked about moving to the next step, an example of an assumptive question is, "When would you like to schedule a time for your tour/appointment/evaluation; would you prefer mornings or afternoons?" This alternative question implies that most callers move to the next level and provides a choice between two selections.

When, Not If

Salespeople on the phone might say something like, "If you'd like to schedule an appointment, I can do that for you" or "You can come in whenever you want; our hours are...."

These two different approaches will yield dramatically different results. The first person will have many customers to meet with; the latter will not.

Great salespeople optimistically believe that the customer will tremendously benefit from their product or service. Once together with the prospective customer, the salesperson signals in at least 10 different ways that he or she expects the customer to buy, hopefully that day.

Bluntly blurting out that you expect your customer to buy from you would be abrupt and pushy. The use of assumptive words and actions, however, will help your customer follow your confident lead.

An example of an assumptive sentence is, "With your purchase today, you will receive a rebate valued at X."

Assumptive words will also help you with repeat business. Repeat business should be much easier to achieve than new business and should be more profitable. A great way to increase the probability of repeat business is by asking, "When would you like to schedule your next visit, would Tuesday or Wednesday be best?" You should ask this question immediately following the completion of the initial service.

Other suggested phrases for assuming the sale:

- "Once you join our family of satisfied clients,…"

- "After you own the (product name), you'll see (benefits)…"

Mrs. Sellmore glanced over and saw that Jack was slumped in his chair again. Wendy either was taking notes or was doodling. With concern, she continued.

Assumptive Actions

"Tom would you give us another specific example of an assumptive action that you use to guide your customer?" Mrs. Sellmore asked.

"Certainly. One example of an assumptive action would be having a filled-out or partially filled out order form," he said. "Also, when you want to take a potential customer from one area to the next in your office, their home, or a showroom, simply take friendly control and gesture while moving toward that area while talking."

"Great point Tom. These are actions that our best producers employ that help guide their customers comfortably through the process," Mrs. Sellmore added.

"If we were selling cars, we should open doors and gesture for clients to get in so they can experience owning the vehicle. Stand back slightly from your office machines or other similar products while motioning and verbally encouraging your clients to step up and push buttons. Hand them things: brochures, samples, color charts, and so on, assuming that they are going to want those things."

The next time you're in a selling situation or have an opportunity to watch one, take note of the assumptive words and actions that the salesperson is employing. Does he or she taking friendly control and if so how? Great performers do.

Lesson 7—Understanding Different Personalities

If you have sales experience, you've probably made what you felt was a great presentation, but you didn't feel that you connected with your prospective customer and, therefore, didn't obtain their trust or business. There's a very valid reason for this.

In sales, you will meet a wide variety of people who will have very different personalities. Great salespeople adjust their overall style (from greeting to closing) to the person/people with whom they are meeting. Most sales-people don't adjust to the personality of their prospective customer. They do the same presentation for everyone and don't understand why some prospects buy from them and others don't.

For centuries, humans have been trying to analyze people and categorize them by personality type. Even ancient Babylonians saw the natural divide of such types and developed one of the earliest personality studies.

Many have found that people divide nicely into four distinct groups. As society and science have advanced, other studies have been conducted and other classifications have developed—and interestingly, four still seems to be the "magic number" for classifying personality types.

Each of the four categories selected represents aspects of an individual's personality. Most people tend to have one dominant type and a secondary, less-dominant style. There is tremendous value in being able to determine both.

In addition to recognizing the personality type of the prospective customer, great salespeople are able to recognize their own personality types. They also work to strengthen the traits they might be lacking that could have a negative impact on their selling abilities.

How to Recognize and Connect with Each Personality Type

The following descriptions are of "prototype" personalities. The majority of the people you work with will seldom exhibit such clear-cut tendencies. But these examples should highlight the key traits of the personality types to help you in identifying them in others and learning how to handle each one.

This information, combined with your mental alertness and instinct, will help your prospective client connect with you.

The Determined Personality

The determined individual likes to be in charge. The determined personality tends to exhibit the following characteristics:

- Cool, impersonal, and in control

- Readily discloses expectations

- Is results-oriented—bottom-line focused

- Risk-taking, competitive, and goal-oriented

- Is time-conscious, gets things done, and makes things happen

- Poor listening skills

- Impatient

- Opinionated

Careers: Often gravitate toward careers where they are in charge such as being business owners, stockbrokers, independent consultants, corporate CEOs, or drill sergeants. Examples are Rudy Guiliani, former mayor of New York City; former British Prime Minister Margaret Thatcher; Donald Trump; and Martha Stewart.

The office of a determined person: The seating is formal, with guest chairs in front of the neat and organized desk. You won't generally see a jar of candy, personal mementos, clipped-out cartoons, or family photos on the desk of the determined professional. The decor suggests power. On the walls might be large planning calendars with deadlines and goals clearly displayed. Awards and honors are often displayed.

Clothing and belongings: Dominant and striking

Relating with the determined personality: To make a more dynamic connection with a determined personality, get to the point as quickly as possible. Offer concise explanations, and focus on outcome rather than the process. This individual wants to know the bottom line: "How is this going to benefit me?" "What's it going to cost me?" "How much money will we make or save?" "When will this project be completed?"

Avoid personal issues, especially theirs. They do not appreciate you getting too close. Suggest ideas for business strategies instead. Do not use pointless humor or engage in small talk ("How was your weekend?"). Stay focused on the topic at hand. Determined personalities do not want to know the long process used to arrive at your conclusion. Sum up the situation, and conclude with a call for action—one that they can delegate.

When looking for ways to reach the determined customer, consider promoting speedy service, bottom-line savings, and solid, no-hassle guarantees.

The Instinctive Personality

The instinctive individual is more of a people person. He or she leads with emotions and values relationships. The instinctive personality is typically as follows:

- Open, unassuming, and receptive

- Reliable and loyal

- A steady worker

- An excellent team player

- Slow to make decisions

- Not time-conscious

- Tends to generalize

- Supportive of others

- Seeks close, first-name basis relationships

- Avoids high-risk situations

Careers: Often found in support roles such as assistants, counseling, teaching, social work, the ministry, psychology, nursing, or human resources. Examples are TV's June Cleaver ("Leave it to Beaver"), newswoman Mary Richards ("The Mary Tyler Moore Show"), and former First Lady Barbara Bush.

The office of an instinctive person: You will see pictures of family and other personal items—and perhaps a jar of candy—on the desk. The walls usually have personal slogans that hang next to more family pictures. The ambience is friendly. Often, the seating is more informal.

Clothing and belongings: Warm, soft, and comfortable

Relating with the instinctive personality: Instinctive people are not impressed by graphs, charts, or long, involved discussions of statistics. While everyone needs some logic to persuade them, instinctive personalities do not need as much. What they *do* need more than most is the ability to relate to and trust you. You will convince these people more effectively with an informal, conversational approach or a group discussion.

Instinctive personalities thrive on contact. Close friends, loyal, long-term customers and clients, and even friendly coworkers may—when appropriate—be open to warm handshakes, back patting, and even hugs.

Persuasive words that instinctives learn by are: Nice, compatible, comfortable, user-friendly, warm, trust, participation, and teamwork.

This individual will be comfortable opening his or her protective territory to allow you to stand closer. He or she responds well to food and gifts. The instinctive customer will also respond well to interest in his or her children or family.

The Visionary Personality

The visionary personality is focused on detail and is concerned with the analytical process. This individual tends to concentrate more on the means rather than on the end. He or she is very logical and very thorough. Other common characteristics of the visionary include:

- Reserved

- Slower to make decisions

- Self-contained

- Good at problem solving and working at solitary tasks

- Learns best by reading

- Hates to be wrong

- Avoids taking risks

- Logical and methodical

Careers: Quality control, accounting, engineering, computer programming, architecture, systems analysis, dentistry, and other technical and hard-science professions. Examples are Mr. Spock of "Star Trek" and Ralph Nader.

The office of a visionary person: A desk covered with neat piles of charts and graphs. Walls, as well, might be covered with evidence of his or her work. Do not expect to find much in the way of personal expression. There will be few family photos or decorative touches. Where is the chair for the visitor placed? The question is not where but *whether* there is a chair at all. This type of personality is task-oriented and focused on work, not entertaining visitors to the office.

Clothing and belongings: Ultra-conservative; pocket protectors are a sure sign.

Relating with the visionary personality: This group of individuals finds it difficult to make decisions if you do not give them a detailed process to follow. The pace of the visionary is likely to be slower than others. Visionary purchasers might take longer to part with their money. Bosses are slower in giving their approval.

They require a great deal of information with statistics to accept a claim. Product ratings, consumer reviews, and solid studies will help speed things up. Normally, visionaries do not welcome physical contact unless they invite it. Limit such contact to handshakes. The visionary hears you better when you use terms such as precise, classified, quantified, qualified, logical, reasoned, facts, specific, figures, trials, tested, and proven.

The Enthusiastic Personality

Enthusiastic personalities are the most flamboyant and emotional types. As the name implies, they are happiest and most productive when they can embrace their jobs with passion and excitement. They are not averse to being in the spotlight and enjoy contact with others. Enthusiastic personalities tend to exhibit the following traits:

- Relationship-oriented

- Open and direct

- Creative

- Crave attention and enjoy being in the spotlight and desire support from others

- Often make quick decisions and are risk-takers and dream-chasers

- Not time-conscious

- Tend to generalize and exaggerate

- Often respond emotionally rather than logically

Careers: Sales, public relations, trial law, and acting. Examples are Jim Carrey, Jonathan Winters, and Johnnie Cochran.

The office of an enthusiastic person: Tends to be cluttered and disorganized. The walls are often covered with inspiring posters expressing motivational slogans. The arrangement will probably be open and friendly with seating arranged so that people can talk easily.

Relating with the enthusiastic personality: Enthusiastic people love the opportunity to talk and perform. Don't bore them with the processes and detailed facts and figures. They don't want to hear it. Straight lecture doesn't bear much fruit with these people. They don't want to listen; rather, they want a high level of involvement and interaction. They want to experience the bells and whistles. If you are selling to an enthusiastic person, make your presentation even more fun than usual and involve the customer. Let him or her open doors, hold the product, or test it out. Get him or her excited.

"By understanding and identifying the personality type or types you are working with, your prospective clients will feel understood and comfortable with you," Mrs. Sellmore said. "When this happens, you will be well on your way to having them accept you and your product or service and reject the offerings from other salespeople's who have not mastered this important philosophy."

Lesson 8—Using Your Instinct to Read Others

Mrs. Sellmore continued, "As we discussed earlier, even though your customers have probably not been trained at interpreting body language, their instincts will be working hard at 'reading you.' Great salespeople realize how much their customers reveal about their feelings without the customer saying a word. It is critical to be able to understand what your customers are saying—non-verbally because they will often only tell you important things like 'I'm ready to buy' non-verbally."

If you work with people and you want to be more successful, you need to develop this 'language' skill. We all have the ability to read these messages. Most people, however, have not taken the time to develop their fluency in reading, interpreting, understanding, and connecting with those around them.

People who are not disciplined in interpreting body language might find it easy to neglect this critical, nonverbal form of communication or pretend that it doesn't exist. Most people are not willing to invest the time or energy to master this pure and powerful form of communication. For those of you who are willing to make the investment, the payoff is astounding.

Reading body language is not as mysterious an art as you might think. It requires more logic and common sense than anything else, because nonverbal communication is simply a physical response to what we are thinking. For example, when you hear a shrieking noise, what do you do? You cover your ears. That is body language. When a child sees a frightening movie, she closes her eyes or covers her head—more body language. Also, when someone knows that she is delivering bad news, without planning she will probably mumble, close her lips, and make the message harder to hear.

Although you would never know it by looking at them, great salespeople watch their customers intensely, interpret the movements of the customer, and then determine how to respond. Sometimes it will be appropriate to keep moving, or sometimes you might need to explain a point further when you see confusion or suspicion. Often, you will only "see," not hear, that the customer is telling you that he or she is ready to buy.

Here are some of the more obvious gestures and their general meanings. You, of course, will need to determine where you are in the sales process and whether the gesture is good or bad. For example, crossed arms are generally negative. The gesture implies being closed or defensive. If you walk into someone's home or office to find her with crossed arms and a scowl, you know that is not good.

The same gesture (in this case, crossed arms)—although still negative—can be an indication of dissatisfaction with their current supplier (the one you would like to replace). Let's say that during qualification, you ask your prospective customer what, if anything, she would like to improve about the service she receives from her current supplier. If she crosses her arms after she begins telling you about how they missed an important deadline, her negativity is directed towards that company, not you.

Here are a few other gestures:

Gesture	Meaning
Rubbing of the neck	Frustration or fatigue
Avoiding eye contact	More interested in something else or being evasive
Hand covering mouth	Uncertainty or possible deceit
Raised eyebrows	Suspicion, disbelief
Eye contact	Interest, respect
Head nodding up and down	Agreement, attentive
Head moving side-to-side	Disagreement
Open hands (palms)	Openness, honesty, willingness to help

Smiling	Positive feelings, openness
Rubbing hands together	Anticipation of something positive for self
Leaning forward	Interest

Steve looked around and noticed Tom's body language. Tom seemed confident and approachable. Steve then glanced over at Jack. Jack was slouched over his chair and looked really bored.

Lesson 9—Anatomy of a Sale

"If you have had any sales training or read any sales books, you probably discovered that making a sale, like many other processes, has an ideal, sequential path," Mrs. Sellmore said. "Teachers have a process for effectively teaching students. Doctors have a process for proper diagnosis and treatment of their patients, and great salespeople also use a process to effectively communicate with their customers. The proper sales sequence is based on the psychology of human, interpersonal communication."

The communication process, as it applies to sales, involves identifying a desire, helping the customer stay open to new ideas, and then presenting the information in a way that is accepted and welcomed.

"Top salespeople consciously understand this process. They are always able to identify the steps while with a customer and to customize each step for maximum efficiency and results within each stage of the sales process," Mrs. Sellmore said, referring again to the slide screen.

A Typical Sales Process

A typical sales process includes the following elements:

- Finding the customer or prospecting for one

- Greeting the customer

- Discovering what the potential customer would like to improve about his or her business or life

- Making an exciting, customized presentation

- Closing—asking for or assuming the business

- Overcoming any objections

"Although it isn't typical, I have included one more step in our process that will increase your performance and income substantially," said Mrs. Sellmore:

- Obtaining referrals

"Your company coaches will now work with you in more detail on these steps providing specific examples and successful techniques that apply to our individual product and your selling environment," she said. "I will check back in on you shortly."

And with that, Mrs. Sellmore wished the trainees well and concluded the session by assigning coaches to each trainee.

"What if we don't want or need a coach?" Jack asked.

While taking a deep breath and trying not to show any frustration with Jack, Mrs. Sellmore responded "Our company believes that every great performer benefits from a mentor or a coach. Top athletes have coaches who help guide them, push them when appropriate, and help them change directions."

With that, the new salespeople all went away separately with the veteran salespeople.

Steve's Coach

Steve was reintroduced to his coach Tom and followed him into his office. Steve noticed a stack of very organized folders.

"What's this?" Steve asked.

"A few concepts and techniques I picked up along my path to success that I'd like to share with you," he said.

"This must have taken you a long time to put together," said Steve.

"I found them necessary and I think you will too. " Tom replied.

"When I begged the CEO for a sales job many years ago, there was no sales manager, training department, or any highly successful salespeople from whom I could obtain guidance," Tom said. "So I read, studied, fumbled quite a bit, and eventually figured out sales for myself. With the training you've already received from Mrs. Sellmore and with any help I can give you, plus a lot of work on your part, I hope you'll be even more successful than I am."

"What do you mean, 'begged' for a sales job?" Steve asked.

"After working as a pilot for a few years, I became bored," Tom said. "I wanted a job in which I could have a dramatic impact. We have a great product at this company. It truly helps people's lives. I wanted to tell as many people as possible about it. I was confident they would love this product as much as I do. My growth seemed capped at my old job. In sales, you are directly rewarded for your efforts. Here, the sky is truly the limit. The profession of sales is honorable—great salespeople truly want the best for others.

I believe that offering a customer a great product or service that will improve his business or personal life is as admirable as a doctor who prescribes medicine to a patient," Tom continued. "Doctors are rewarded both financially and in job satisfaction for their knowledge and ability to help others' lives. So are we."

"You're telling me you actually gave up a career as a pilot to become a salesperson?" Steve asked in amazement.

"It was the best move I ever made," Tom said proudly.

Steve recalled that Tom was one of the salespeople whose name had been shown on the screen during training and remembered how much money he was earning. With that in mind, Steve was determined to listen to and embrace any and all the knowledge that Tom could share.

Lesson 10—Networking

Steve listened attentively to Tom's coaching. "The biggest challenge most salespeople have is finding enough customers to present their terrific product or service to. Great salespeople realize that every day they are surrounded by an abundance of people who are potential clients. These great salespeople understand the importance of always cultivating a base of people they can contact and tell about new products or services they are involved with," he said.

"Beyond your friends or relatives, think about all the other people you know," Tom said. "For example, sport teams, clubs, community groups, church groups, etc. Our company belongs to the local Chamber of Commerce. Their meetings are a great place to meet people who either are right for our product or who know the right person in their company or in other companies who will benefit from our product. The chamber even provides a directory with more companies than you can count."

"We also belong to Toastmasters™, an organization dedicated to the fine art of public speaking," Tom said. "It's a terrific organization. They have lots of fun, challenging, and enlightening experiences. You will meet many nice and supportive people there."

"Remember to give to these organizations, rather than just taking," he said. "See what service you can provide the other members with. Like many other organizations and companies, we participate in community service programs. Making time to help with these projects is a great way to do a good deed and have an opportunity to get to know other great people better."

Tom continued, "Great salespeople are always networking and follow what I describe as the three-foot rule. Anyone who comes within three feet of me could become a customer. All I need to do is say 'hello' and start a pleasant conversation. Just last week I closed a sale from someone I met in an elevator. Even if that person hadn't been right for our product, I would have asked him about his activities and who in those groups might have a need for our product. If the person you're talking with isn't a potential client today, they probably know someone who is or might become a potential client in the future. So, with that in mind, literally everyone can help you in some way, and is usually willing, if you ask the right way. By that I mean that you approach everyone with an attitude of servitude. Always ask, 'What can I do for you?' Don't expect everyone to answer with a need that our product or service fulfills. It could be that they need information, advice or a contact with someone *you* know. Most people feel obligated to help you in some way if you help them. If you begin with obliging them, you'll receive more benefits back than if you start by approaching them with wanting something from them, such as their business.

I encourage you to implement the same strategy of other top salespeople. They exchange 10 business cards a day with people they meet during their normal routines," Tom said.

"This way of approaching people may initially intimidate you, Steve. So, I will give you strategies to do it professionally and to overcome the fear of rejection in a little while. Fear is one of the biggest obstacles that stands in the way of sales success. We have to get it out of the way to become our best at networking."

Lesson 11—Getting as Many Appointments as Possible

After checking in with the other teams, Mrs. Sellmore joined Tom and Steve as Tom continued. "As I mentioned, the most difficult thing for any business is finding new customers," he said. "New customers come to you two ways— they find you or you find them. In our business, a sale comes after an appointment. Imagine the sales process to be like a funnel. The sales come out the small end. Someone has to fill the large opening of the funnel with leads. Rather than wait for the customers to come to them, great salespeople have honed their prospecting skills to keep appointments flowing."

Mrs. Sellmore added, "When I was in retail sales and business was slow, I often called existing clients to get new prospects. I received some of my best customers this way."

Various Ways to Contact Prospects

Tom added, "There are various ways to reach prospective customers, including stopping in unannounced, direct mail, e-mail, or the telephone. The best way to communicate and motivate anyone is in a face-to-face situation. The most effective way to set up a face-to-face appointment is by using the telephone."

Outbound Calls

"You mean cold calling?" Steve asked.

Tom responded, "Did you ever play the guessing game hot and cold? You know, when you got closer to the right area you got warmer and the farther away you were colder. That's an appropriate description of cold calling. Cold calling is contacting anyone and everyone, hoping they will have some interest in your product. I've certainly made my share of sales from cold calling, but this strategy alone can be exhausting.

So rather than searching for a needle in a haystack, I prefer to go to the right haystack—people who we have some connection to or people we have a reason to believe will benefit from our product. That's warm prospecting," Tom said.

"To do this, think about all the people you already know who will benefit from our product," he continued. "Start with your friends and relatives who are in a field that could benefit from our product. This is a very comfortable place to start. They will be supportive and understanding—a great practice field. After all these years, I still have many customers today that I can trace back to that first list of friends and relatives."

Steve wrote in his journal:

> Make a list of friends or relatives that will benefit from my product.

What to say

Most people, especially people you know, will want to help you when you ask for their assistance. It's really pretty simple and may go something like this:

You: Hi, John, this is Tom, how are you?

John: I'm good Tom, how are you?

You: I'm terrific, John. I just took a job with a great company—the ABC Company that makes fantastic (widgets) that save people/companies (a lot of time each day) and increases (their enjoyment/productivity). I really think it's exciting and because I value your opinion, I'd love to stop by tomorrow and show it to you. Is the morning or the afternoon better for you?

John: Gee, Tom, tomorrow isn't good.

You: Would Wednesday or Thursday be better?

John: Thursday afternoon is good.

You: Great, I could pop by at 2:00 or would 3:30 P.M. be better for you?

John: 3:30 works.

You: Great, I look forward to seeing you then.

If you are determined to become highly successful in sales, you will take responsibility for filling the funnel and spend up to 75 percent of your day getting in front of people who will benefit from your product. That's what someone who is new to sales must do in order to achieve success in this field. Proven salespeople spend a minimum of 15 percent of their time prospecting—even when they think that they have enough business.

Business to Business—Getting to the Decision Maker

"If we don't know the name and title of the person who makes the decisions to purchase our product or service within a company, we need to find that out for ourselves," Tom said. "Then, we need to contact this person. This can be difficult as most decision-makers are frequently away from their desks traveling to meetings or on other calls. That is where the help of the receptionist comes in."

"I would think receptionists would keep salespeople away from their bosses," Steve asked.

Receptionist—Friend or Foe?

Tom smiled and answered, "Most people, including receptionists, don't like pushy, unkind people. However, they much more often than not will be nice to people and provide assistance when asked by a person who treats them with the respect and kindness they deserve."

Most salespeople don't appreciate how valuable a receptionist can be in helping them succeed. Receptionists are the people who know what each employee's area of responsibility is in order to direct calls properly, so they can be a great help. A few suggestions when you talk with receptionists are to:

- Smile. A smile can be "heard" over the phone.

- Be highly respectful and courteous.

- Use their first name—ask for it if they did not volunteer it.

- Ask for their help.

- Clarify all the information that you want before being transferred.

Here is an example:

Receptionist: Sunset Sail Company, where can I direct your call?

You: Hi, my name is Steve, may I ask your name please?

Receptionist: This is Mary, how may I help you?

You: Mary, I really could use your help. What is the name of the person who is responsible for purchasing (widgets) for your company?

Receptionist: That would be Mark Smith. He's not available at the moment. I can transfer you to his voice mail so you may leave him a message.

You: Mary, before you do would you please tell me his extension number and the best time to reach him?

Mrs. Sellmore added, "Receptionists often know more about the people in a company than most other people. Once you establish rapport, you can ask a wide range of questions including whether this person has an assistant, his/her hours, name, current vendors the company is working with, and so on. By using the approach that you need help and are not demanding anything, you will be amazed at how much valuable information you can gain."

Once You Know the Decision-Maker's Name...

"Once you know the decision-maker's name, you can get past 'blocks' (as they are often called) by using a confident voice and few words. For example, when calling the ABC company, the receptionist answers: 'ABC company, can I help you?' Your response is, 'Yes, John Stevens please.' When she asks who's calling, state only your name—making certain your ending tone is down at the end. Remember when we talked about 'voice' in class? You need to sound confident. I cannot tell you how many top executives I have spoken with who have told me they were surprised I got through to them. Their receptionist thought that I was someone important who they already knew."

Working with the Decision-Maker's Assistant

The assistant's job is to save his or her boss as much time as possible, which includes blocking any unnecessary calls. Your job is to present your call as one of the important ones. Being referred by someone is a very effective way of doing just that.

If you strike out with the assistant, try reaching the boss when the assistant isn't at his/her desk. This is where that information we received from the receptionist comes in handy again. Try the decision-maker's direct extension during hours that many assistants are away from their desk, including before 8 A.M., lunch, and after 5 P.M.

Once you reach your prospective client

- Smile.

- Speak clearly and have an enthusiastic greeting, such as "Good morning" or "Good afternoon."

- Introduce yourself and your company.

- Tell them who referred you to call them (inside or outside of the company) or whether you are a customer.

- Use a question that should solicit a positive response, such as, "I have been told that you are the person in charge of maximizing office efficency, is that correct?"

- Be direct and tell them what you can do to make their life better. "My job is increasing the productivity of employees and saving companies money by mimimizing down time."

- Assume the appointment. Ask the customer to choose which of two days or times is better for an an appointment. "Which is a better day for us to meet: Tuesday or Wednesday?"

- Confirm the appointment.

- Thank them. Then, get off the phone.

- Call your receptionist/friend to get directions or other information with which the decision-maker does not need to occupy his or her time.

Lesson 12—Overcoming the Fear of Rejection

As we discussed earlier, fear is one of the largest obstacles in a salesperson's path to success. Fear can be reduced by implementing a few powerful and proven strategies.

Practice

"OK, let's do a little role playing," said Tom. "I'll be the receptionist, and you try to get through to the decision maker."

"Role playing?" Steve winced.

"Yes," he said. "Role-playing is one of the best ways to work out the kinks in your sales process. It allows you to stumble in a safe environment. At first, it feels awkward—even silly, but it works."

"I understand your discomfort," Mrs. Sellmore added. "However, think about how much Sammy Sosa, Tiger Woods, or Michael Jordan practiced to become top performers. If you've read anything about them, you know they've spent countless hours practicing their disciplines. Sales is a discipline as well. It deserves the same kind of commitment. How much money does the average professional baseball player, basketball player, or golfer make? A lot! Why? They practice! The same goes for professional salespeople."

"Practice can help you enforce important skills such as tone of voice, articulation, expressions, body language, and your choice of words," she said. "Practicing will also reduce your fear of the competition and of rejection. Unmanaged fear destroys success. Great salespeople aggressively work to eliminate it."

Steve wrote in his sales journal:

Practice — A Lot

"I guess you're right," Steve said, "but I'm still uncomfortable."

"You're at a pivotal point, Steve," he said. "Many people know what they should do, but most just don't do it for one reason or another. One of those reasons is, believe it or not, the fear of rejection or the fear of success! One of the best ways to overcome the fear of rejection is to practice. When you practice, you desensitize yourself. People who aren't afraid to be successful figure out what needs to be done and they do it, no matter how it makes them feel at the time." Steve thought about how interns and new doctors have to go for days with little sleep but still "give it their all" when a patient needs them.

If you have a fear of success, that's another issue that must be addressed. You'll have to work on believing that you deserve the rewards this profession can bring you and it's all based on serving others. Remember, the income you earn in sales is nothing more than a mirror reflection of the quantity and quality of service you provide.

"You'll do many things in sales that'll make you feel awkward at first, including asking for your customer's business or asking for referrals," Tom said. "The question is, 'Are you going to let fear get in your way?'"

"Great salespeople often devote a minimum of 10 percent of their professional week to practicing," he said. "They practice a part or parts of the sales process with a colleague, a manager, or just by themselves in front of a mirror. You can even have someone videotape you so you can see first-hand how you come across to others. Thirty-second television commercials are often filmed and edited for dozens of hours and involve many retakes to get it just right. They are selling themselves—and so are you."

Persistence

"Persistence is the ability to face defeat again and again without giving up—to push on in the face of great difficulty," Tom continued. "Persistence means taking pains to overcome every obstacle, to do all that is necessary to reach our goals."

Athletes have to endure *physical* pain and *injury* to improve their performance and reach their goals. Although most salespeople will not have to endure physical pain, to be successful they will have to get past emotional vulnerability and discomfort. Salespeople who want to become successful need to realize that they have no reason to expect to be successful with a new technique or presentation at first. Similarly, a long distance runner doesn't clear a hurdle or have his best time the first day that he runs.

"I still feel awkward doing any role playing," Steve said.

"That's normal," Tom said. "The first time you do this, you'll probably laugh at yourself—and that's good! Humility is a virtue, and most people find it very human and endearing. After you stop laughing, though, and get back to business, you'll be able to critique your facial expressions, your body language, your tone of voice, and your overall presentation. Dan Rather, Katie Couric, or any great television personality practiced to become what they are today."

"Great point!" Steve said. "Let's go!"

With a few starts and stops, Steve was able to successfully set an appointment with Tom and felt confident he was able to find people to speak with about his product.

Lesson 13—Great Greetings

After a short break, Tom, Mrs. Sellmore, and Steve reconvened. Steve had seen Wendy and Jack during the break. Wendy seemed excited to finally be getting close to making her own sales, although she still was nervous about how much work she still had to do. Jack's attitude was still the same as before: "This stuff may help new salespeople, but I don't need it. I know what I'm doing."

"By this time, Steve, you look great, you sound confident, and you are about to meet your prospective customer," Mrs. Sellmore began. "Let's establish the goal of the greeting. When a salesperson greets customers who have come into a store and left their own office or home environment, the customers' anxiety levels are generally high. People do not move forward easily if they are anxious or uncomfortable. Therefore, your goals of the greeting are to:

- Reduce the customer's anxiety by making them feel comfortable

- Exhibit a credible presence—laying the foundation to allow them to trust you

Contact, Common Ground, and Compliments

Here are the steps to a great greeting:

- **Smile** with a sincere, "It's good to meet you" smile.

- **Contact**
  - **Eye contact**. Although you will be nervous and maybe even a little intimidated, especially if you perceive this person as very important, remember that eye contact shows interest and confidence. The lack of eye contact shows a lack of confidence and possibly deceit.

  - **Physical contact.** Offer a confident handshake. Remember to have an open, slightly face-up palm. While shaking someone's hand, do not try to break their hand, but make certain your grip is full and confident.

- **Set an upbeat tone** while exchanging names. The handshake is the perfect and most natural time to do this. Enthusiastically say "Good morning." Offer your name,

"Steve Saunders." Say, "It's great to meet you." Wait for their name, and listen for correct pronunciation (including whether they shorten their name). Only call Robert "Bob" if he introduces himself that way first.

- If you have an appointment, **proceed to where you will be having your meeting** if you were not already shown there.

- **Ask a question** to get them to open up and begin telling you about themselves. For example: "John, how long have you been with Nordic Enterprises?" or "What brought you to this company?"

- **Find common ground.** People will do business easier with people they feel comfortable with. Try to find something that you have in common. Depending on what dominant personality type you believe this person to be, decide whether the common ground will be the referral source, a sports team displayed, or family pictures in the office.

- **Compliments**—When you meet someone, consciously look for something you like about that person. While doing so, you will often find something that you *sincerely* like. Tell him or her so through a sincere compliment.

Begin by telling him or her directly and clearly why you are there and what you are going to do for them.

Tom added, "These steps might seem a bit straightforward, but believe us, Steve, when we tell you that every little nuance in sales will impact your bottom line."

Lesson 14—Qualifying

Mrs. Sellmore asked Steve, "Do you think salespeople should spend more time talking about the product or the person they are with?"

"Probably both!" Steve reluctantly replied.

"All salespeople go into a sales call and face this prover- bial fork in the road," Mrs. Sellmore said. "Weak and aver- age salespeople are thrilled to head down the product path and get right into talking about their product, because that's where they're comfortable. Whether they mean to or not, they seem to 'push' their product on people. They somehow feel secure in product discussions because they can get their arms around statistics and facts. They realize they don't know much about the people involved. Although counter-intuitive, the best approach is to get to know the people and their situation *first*, then discuss the product once you determine which product will resolve their needs."

By doing so, your customer will be more willing to accept your assistance and advice. Assistance and advice will follow in the presentation stage.

Our goal in the qualification stage is to:

- Identify the desires and needs that the prospective customer is aware he or she has

- Uncover the areas the customer might not yet realize that he or she has

- Create a sense of urgency

"Great salespeople know their products and services inside and out but spend more time on the people path," Mrs. Sellmore said. "They talk about their products, but only after they truly understand their customer—what he wants and why he wants it. Then, a great salesperson explains in an exciting way—how, when, and why their product or company meets each customer's needs."

"So, how do I figure out what a customer wants?" Steve asked.

"Great salespeople are more concerned about being inter-est*ed* than interest*ing*," Mrs. Sellmore said. "They have prepared and practiced a list of great questions. The goal of your questions is to learn what your customer needs instead of assuming that you know and merely blabbing about your product. This strategy is based on the great philosopher, Socrates, and his method of dialog. This is the same strategy taught to doctors, professors, and other important, credible professions."

"How can Socrates help me become a better salesperson?" Steve asked, puzzled.

Selling with Socrates

Mrs. Sellmore continued, "The Socratic method of teaching by asking questions[11] helps customers participate and buy-in to finding a solution or answer to their problem. When used properly, it will help your customers understand how much they truly will benefit from your product and help you to overcome your most common and difficult objections, including price.

This technique enables the person you are speaking with to draw logical conclusions rather than having them forced by you.

Great professors will get their points across to students by asking them questions in a sequential manner, not by lecturing to them.

Learning to ask questions in a genuine and caring manner will enable you to help your customer realize how the purchase of a needed item is more important than any short-term discomfort from the price of that item. A great salesperson knows how to use the Socratic Method of questioning in order to more effectively communicate with the customer."

"Let's say that you're selling lawn tractors," Mrs. Sellmore said. "You pull up to a customer's house and find him cutting a fairly large lawn with a push mower. Based on your experience and knowledge, you're able to approximate the square footage and the typical rate of speed at which a person can push a mower, and you calculate that it must take your prospective customer three hours to cut the lawn.

If you said, 'I've done my homework and I figure it takes you three hours to cut your lawn,' your customer probably would feel trapped by a pushy salesman and reject you and your product or service.

But instead, after the proper greeting and building common ground, telling him about or showing him your references, you *asked* how long it takes to cut the lawn and he said, 'Oh, about three hours.' Then, those three hours are somehow more real to him and probably quite irritating. Then you could ask whether he would like to reduce this time or if he would be interested in a product that could cut the mowing time in half. His answer probably would be 'Yes.' Then you can talk about your product and how it can help cut down the lawn-cutting time. Great salespeople tend to ask questions, rather than blab about their products."

"What questions should I ask?" Steve asked, intrigued.

Great Questions

Mrs. Sellmore states, "Start by thinking logically and sequentially. For starters, if a customer comes into your place of business, I would want to find out why he's there. I prefer to find out this information and simultaneously establish my company as a leader by asking, 'Who referred you to us?' This implies that most people are referred to us."

"Since you can't read a customer's mind—just ask," she said. "Most salespeople are afraid to ask customers a lot of questions. Great salespeople realize customers love to talk about themselves, and proper questions get the ball rolling."

Top salespeople have a list of great, well thought-out questions that heighten the customer's sense of urgency. Within each industry, a sales professional should have dozens of valuable questions to ask each prospective customer. After the salesperson compiles such a list, she should memorize it.

List as many questions as possible that will reveal your customer's desires. In other words, what is going on in your customer's life that requires improvement or change?

Here are some questions that great salespeople use:

Uncovering Why Customers Are Considering Your Product or Service and Understanding Urgency

- How long have you been considering contacting us?

- What made you decide to stop in and see us *now*?

Uncover Current Options

- What are you currently using?

- Where did you find your current (item)?

- How did you end up with that (item)?

- How did you choose the company you purchased it from?

- What do you like about that company?

- Is there anything you don't like about it?

- How pleased have you been with the performance or the reliability of your current product/service?

- What happens when your product needs service?

- Who is most affected by it?

- Why are you replacing it?

- What are you hoping your new product will do that your current product does not?

- What great things have you heard about the new (item)?

- What is most important to you when purchasing a new (so and so)?

- How soon would you like to be benefiting from a new (so and so)?

- Are independent (*safety/reliability* reports) important to you?

The Company

- Who referred you to our company?

- What great things have you heard about our company?

- Who do you know who has one of our products?

- How familiar are you with our product or company?

- Is the number of years a company has been in business important to you?

- Is technical support after you have invested in a product important to you?

- What kind of support would you like?

The Experts

- Is quality something that is important to you?

- Is it important for you to deal with experts when it comes to this product?

- Are the opinions of independent experts important to you?

Price

- Will you be making your decision today based solely on price?

- When making a decision such as this one, what is most important to you: price, quality, or excellent support?

Steve was amazed. "Wow, aren't those a lot of questions?"

"Not if you ask them in an interested, non-threatening and conversational way," Tom said. "You're not grilling or interrogating the potential client for information. You're asking appropriate questions based on the answers they provide as the conversation progresses. Your goal is to get a very clear picture of their desires or needs."

Just as a doctor needs to ask the appropriate questions to diagnose patients, great salespeople need to do the same. Beginning questions with who, what, when, where, and why are called open-ended questions. Their answers require some thought on the part of the potential client and therefore get the customer to open up. The answers should help you determine your next question to move the sale forward.

Other types of questions are called closed-ended questions. These are questions that do not require a lot of thought and can possibly be answered by reflex or with one or two words. These questions have value because they often require a decision and help narrow down and speed up the selection process. For example, "John, where would you prefer the product be delivered?" "Mary, what date do you feel would be best for the training class on the product?"

Another type of question is called the alternative choice question. This question has two choices. Either choice provides you with important information or moves the sale forward. They could be simple 'yes' or 'no' questions that help you eliminate a line of thought that you might have had about a product or service to meet the customer's needs. Or, you can use this question as a closing question, such as: "John, I can arrange for delivery of your new (widget) on Thursday afternoon, or would Saturday morning be better for you?" You have provided two choices, and neither requires a lot of thought.

Another type of question to move toward agreement is the tie-down. This strategy involves making a statement you think the customer will agree to, then tying it down with a question. For example, "A reputation for professionalism is important, isn't it?" The phrase "isn't it" is the tie-down. Not many customers would disagree with that statement. You have accomplished two things with this method: 1) you have implied that your company has that reputation for professionalism, and 2) the customer has agreed with you. Each minor agreement helps build their confidence in making a positive decision.

Regardless of the type of question you ask, remember to focus on the answers to the questions and their meanings rather than just moving on to your next question.

Steve wrote in his journal:

"Great salespeople focus on being interested (in the customer) more than sounding interesting and have mastered asking a powerful quality and quantity of questions."

Lesson 15—Shutting Down the Competition

Mrs. Sellmore added, "There is another category that we don't want to leave out. This category, as well, may seem counter-intuitive.

Top salespeople pro-actively uncover other options or companies a potential customer is considering and offers to compare and contrast the differences for the customer early on in the sales process. We are not afraid of other companies in our industry; we are prepared to deal with them. Customers find this confidence refreshing and appealing."

"You don't actually want me to ask a customer if he or she is planning on shopping around, do you?" Steve asked with disbelief.

"Only if you want to be a great salesperson," she said. Weak salespeople are afraid to ask about other options or companies. Then, after their presentations and when they ask for the business, they are often disappointed when customers tell them they are going to look around. If you learn about other companies at the end, it is extremely difficult to recover and get the sale. A great question to uncover other options or companies the customer is considering that I recommend you use early on is:

- What other options and/or companies are you considering that I can compare and contrast for you today?

Most salespeople don't ask these types of questions because they are afraid that by asking, they're telling a customer that there *are* other options, and because of that the customer might choose one or more of those options. In our industry, and in most industries, the customer would have to be a fool not to know that there are other options.

Not talking about other options creates confusion because the customer is often spending mental energy wondering how other companies stack up and if they should shop around—therefore, building buying resistance.

"Asking what other options your customer is considering shows that you realize there are other products on the market (although not necessarily equal) and shows complete confidence and openness on your part to discuss those options with the customer," Mrs. Sellmore said. "This approach is refreshing and powerful!"

"Got it," Steve said, as he wrote in his journal:

Uncover other options or companies my customer is considering up front, rather than being surprised later when they tell me they have to think about it or shop around.

"Once you uncover that a customer is considering another company, you can customize your presentation, highlighting why, based on all of the other information you have uncovered about his or her desires during the qualification stage, your product is best for their situation," Mrs. Sellmore said.

Remember, great salespeople never say anything negative about another company's products—nor do they mention another company by name, because it seems defensive and will probably work against them. You are not an expert on another company's product. The customer knows that and probably won't believe anything that you have to say about another company's product. We are not suggesting that you don't investigate other company's products or services. Knowing about other products will help you identify and then emphasize our competitive superiority to your customer. Great salespeople can highlight their superiority without saying a bad word about any other company.

"Often, when a customer tells a salesperson about other options he or she is considering, and the salesperson responds properly and non-defensively, the customer will undoubtedly be impressed with the salesperson's professionalism and confidence and more often than not, buy from them," Mrs. Sellmore said.

"What's a good response?" asked Steve.

Response Once You Confirm Your Customer Is Considering Other Options

"You can say something like, 'I'm glad you're interested in providing your (family) with the (highest safety). During our brief time together, I will compare and contrast the many differences, show you why our product is superior—especially in your situation, and why we may be a (bit more expensive),'" Mrs. Sellmore advised.

"Wow!" exclaimed Steve. "You want to tell a customer up front you're going to be more expensive than other companies?"

"Yes, because if I wait until the end, it's essentially guaranteed that the customer will have to think about it and shop around," she said. "If you address it up front, at the least he or she will have time to adjust to the concept that your product will cost more money and be listening to why it is more expensive. Then based on everything your customer has seen and heard from you, your customer will decide if it's worth the additional investment. Your customer will listen more carefully to why. If you do a fabulous, exciting, customized presentation, the customer probably will decide that yours is the better product even if it does cost a bit more."

Steve wrote in his journal:

> "Great salespeople are able to have clear, direct conversations with their customers."

"While qualifying, you can also ask questions that will help your customer see a value in 'add-on' products. Going back to the lawn mower, here are some more questions you could ask Mr. Jones," Mrs. Sellmore said.

- Are you interested (in a tool) that can also (trim your garden areas effortlessly and safely)?

- Are you interested in minimizing the hazards associated with your current option?

- Would you like to cut your cleanup time in half?

"What if they don't answer the question in the way you hope?" asked Steve.

"That's OK," she said. "The customer is still thinking about the issue you're presenting. Just move on. If you truly are interested in what your customer wants, you'll find that your customer will eventually give you the information you need."

"When something doesn't make sense to you, simply blame yourself. Explain to the customer you're confused or must have missed something and ask the customer to clarify what you don't understand."

"Never interrupt a customer however, even when the customer is interrupting you. What comes out of a customer's mouth is almost always golden. I've heard countless salespeople interrupt a customer and cost themselves a sale. Beyond simply bad manners, interrupting stops the momentum and gives the customer a reason to delay the purchase."

Steve wondered whether he interrupted people and wrote:

"Don't interrupt the customer—be highly respectful."

How and Why to Create a Sense of Urgency

Great salespeople realize that it is their job to uncover and heighten their customer's sense of urgency. Without creating a sense of urgency, you will probably end up giving a good presentation but the customer will not buy from you then, or maybe not at all. Without pushing, great salespeople help the customer understand what might be lost (or not gained) by not moving ahead with the solution. Great questions can help you gently build a sense of urgency.

"Let's say that you are selling energy-efficient windows," Mrs. Sellmore said. "What would a typical customer want to improve about his or her life that would heighten the sense of urgency toward buying energy efficient windows?"

"Lower utility bills?" Steve suggested.

"Exactly," she said. "So, rather than *telling* the customer that you can reduce their monthly gas or electric payment, great salespeople use the Socratic Method and *ask* the customer about current payments—getting the customer to focus on that bill. Then, help the customer do the calculations of what that customer could save. In an excited yet non-arrogant way, ask the customer whether he would like some help saving, for example, $50 every month—or better yet, say $600 a year or tell him that you would like to help him do so."

"Once you have compiled all of this incredibly valuable—even golden—information that the customer gave you, tuck the information away in your mental treasure chest so you can customize the presentation exactly to what the customer wants."

Lesson 16—Powerful Presentations

"What is the goal of the presentation part of the sale?" Mrs. Sellmore asked.

"To tell the customer about our product?" Steve responded with hesitation.

"That's what most salespeople think, and they end up boring their customers to tears with mundane facts and figures," she replied. "Great, well-trained salespeople, however, stay away from product-focused presentations. They understand that their job is to deliver an exciting, inspiring, motivating, and most important—customer-customized presentation. *They are constantly thinking about and presenting information from the customer's perspective and answering the customer's constant question, 'Why is this important to me?'* When this type of presentation is done properly, the cost of the product will be outweighed by the value of the customer owning your product."

The goal of the presentation is to help motivate the customer to move forward by giving him or her the solution to identified wants and needs in a way he or she is interested in and willing to accept. This process is no different from a doctor writing a prescription for a patient in pain. To accept your recommendations and move forward, however, your customer needs to trust that you are an expert and that your company is capable and proven.

Most salespeople agree that "exciting" and "trust" are good but never consciously think about implementing ways to make themselves and their presentations more exciting and themselves and their company more trusted. There are many ways to make your product or service more fascinating. We have already talked about two of them: tone of voice and using effective body language. To demonstrate trustworthiness, you should look the part of an expert professional, act that way, and have testimonials available from satisfied clients.

"The next key to a successful presentation is what you say to a customer," Mrs. Sellmore said. "Some salespeople, like us, are fortunate enough to have a sales presentation guide with a script that provides us with the most credible, concise, compelling, and competitive message in a sequential, logical manner."

Great sales presentation guides are created and tested by expert sales trainers. Salespeople who are not provided with a sales presentation guide need to create their own version. It should also contain a concise, compelling, and competitive presentation of your strengths and superiorities that answer your customer's desires. The format should be succinct and sequential, with captivating images that are identifiable to your prospective customer.

Weak salespeople often view sales presentation guides as a crutch. They think that they are above using such a tool and will sound phony or rehearsed. Other salespeople who do not have a sales presentation guide and script often bounce around like ping-pong balls and have random discussions with their customers, creating customer confusion. Customers generally do not move forward and purchase products when they are confused.

A great sales presentation is filled with customer benefits. Most weak salespeople like blabbing about their products' features. Features are specific characteristics of the product. Benefits, however, are what the customer gets from a feature. Customers care about benefits more than about features. You will see that the sales presentation guide script is filled with benefit statements that begin with phrases like, "So, what this means to you is…" We know that we need to deliver the information from the customer's perspective.

"Without a sales presentation guide, salespeople need to present information about themselves, their company, and their past performance so that the customer sees them as credible experts," Mrs. Sellmore advised.

"How is that done?" Steve asked.

"Because most people learn best visually, plaques, pictures, awards, and/or letters of recommendation from other customers are always helpful," she said. "Referral letters should be on the satisfied client's own letterhead or in his or her own writing to be the most credible."

Pace of the Sale

The speed at which you present information to a customer helps the customer listen better, relate to, and appreciate your message more.

"Being too fast or too slow will frustrate a customer," Mrs. Sellmore said. "In my experience, however, most salespeople cover things too slowly, and bore their customers.

"The first thing a great salesperson should do is notice his or her customer's pace. You will find that a results-orientated customer will generally speak faster than a detail-oriented person. Rather than merely matching your prospect's pace, however, speed up just a little.

Remember, people generally can listen to a far greater number of words per minute than you can speak. The pace of someone who is confident is generally more brisk than that of someone less confident. Having a brisk pace creates excitement. When your pace is brisk, your prospective customer will work a little harder to listen to you."

"That's good." Steve commented.

"That's very good," answered Tom.

"If a customer has to spend a little more mental energy focusing and listening to you, he will undoubtedly have to block out other distractions and, hopefully, will get caught up in your excitement," he said.

Steve wrote:

"Speed up!"

Vocabulary of a Great Salesperson

"Let's move on to the best vocabulary," Mrs. Sellmore continued.

As with any profession, sales has certain words that are heard frequently in the industry. Unfortunately, many of the common terms used by salespeople bring about negative images in the minds of potential clients. The word "pitch" is one of many negative words used within the sales profession.

Negative words and phrases lead to the reduction of respect and credibility to an individual as well as the overall profession of sales. We suggest you use words that create respect and positive images in the minds of our clients.

Pitch is defined in the dictionary[12] as "To attempt to promote or sell, often in a high-pressure manner." Instead of using the word pitch, true professionals call this process a presentation or an exchange of information based on the customer's desires.

Another negative word is "spiel." A spiel[13] is defined as "a talk or harangue; harangue defined as a 'long, blustering speech; a tirade.'"[14] Great salespeople do not want to harangue their customers, so they avoid the word "spiel" and replace it with "discussion."

These are a few other words to avoid when with a prospective client:

Words to Avoid	Better Replacements
Quote, Estimate, Bid	Proposal
Package	Choices
Deal	Opportunity
Contract	Agreement
Objection	Question
You're wrong/No	Actually…

Cost or price	Investment
Monthly payment	Monthly investment
Customers	People we serve
Words to Avoid	*Better Replacements*
Commission	Fee for service
Appointment *(in consumer sales)*	Visit
Buy	Own
Sign	OK, approve, endorse, authorize
Cheaper	More economical
Sell or sold	Get them involved, help them acquire
Prospect	Potential future client
Problems	Challenges

By replacing demeaning, unprofessional words with professional vocabulary, we garner more respect from our potential clients, satisfied clients, and coworkers, and we feel better about ourselves. Regardless of whether your client uses slang, the use of slang by a salesperson gives that client an indication of a low level of professionalism.

Last, be careful not to use trade or industry talk when speaking with someone outside of or not familiar with your industry. Clients might not understand or appreciate it, and you *never* want to cause confusion in the mind of the potential client.

Adjectives

Using powerful, exciting adjectives is another way of making you and your presentation exciting.

Steve remembered learning how important it was to answer in strong adjectives, such as saying, "I'm *great*" or "Things are *outstanding*" when replying to the question, "How are you?"

"When you role-played with me before, do you remember using many adjectives?" Tom asked.

"Not really," Steve responded.

"Actually, you used a few. Great salespeople use a lot of adjectives, because they are sincerely enthusiastic about their product and what they believe the product will do for the client. Let's make a list of as many exciting adjectives as we can that describe our product," Tom suggested.

Modern	Programmable
Computerized	Revolutionary
Sleek	Digital
Lightweight	Striking

State-of-the-art	Cutting-edge
Sophisticated	Versatile
Compact	Water-resistant

"Adjectives help tip the scale of value and begin to out-weigh the investment factor," Tom said. "Whenever possible, quantify the adjectives that you use. For example, instead of saying 'recommended by doctors,' if you say 'recommended by over 1,000 leading doctors nationwide,' it will make your presentation more credible and impressive."

Getting the Customer Involved— Questions and Movement

Another strategy to keep your potential client involved in your presentation is to end each product description with a question. For example, after you have begun explaining the quality of, let's say, the leather in your product, ask your potential client how he or she likes the quality of the leather or which color he or she would like best. Then, move on to the next point without too much of a pause.

Pausing too long enables your customer's mind to default to counterproductive thoughts. For example, he or she might think about running behind schedule, what is going on back at work, or dwelling on the price.

Also, great salespeople get their customers physically involved. Hand them things like swatches, color samples, charts, and graphs and get them into the driver's seat. Let them push buttons open and close doors and drawers for themselves. When customers take physical possession of some part of a product or service, it is easier for them to envision taking physical possession of the product itself.

Salespeople who sell fabric couches often also sell a fabric-coating system that protects against staining from spills. One way to get potential clients to see the value of the product is to tell them about it. Another is for the salesperson to pour liquid on a treated fabric, showing how the liquid runs off. The most effective approach, however, is leading potential clients to actually perform the demonstration themselves. This activity will be the most convincing and most impressive to them. They will believe it more if they do it themselves.

Ethics

It is important to excite your potential clients with a motivating presentation but never to mislead them. Great salespeople are ethical people. No product is perfect. Potential clients understand that. When you are honest with them about any perceived limitations regarding your product, your potential clients will trust you more. Just as doctors prescribe prescriptions, they also let patients know about possible side effects and any possible ways they can avoid the unpleasant effects. This reason is part of why they are trusted.

Salespeople should follow the same standard. If an equipment warranty is included with your product but not a labor warranty, be sure the potential client understands the distinction and how to avoid or minimize labor charges. This honesty might even create an opportunity of offering a supplemental maintenance or warranty coverage program.

There might be times when you'll have to walk away from a potential sale because the product is not a good fit for your potential client.

Steve wrote in his book:

"Great salespeople are honest and don't mislead their clients."

"Are there any other areas, besides misleading a potential client, that I should avoid?" Steve inquired.

"Yes, there are several common presentation errors."

Common Presentation Errors

Taking Shortcuts

If a professional athlete cuts corners in training and tries to rush the process, he or she will quickly feel the physical pain of that decision. Untrained or undisciplined salespeople feel the similar pain of losing sales almost every day but generally do not take the time to figure out why it's happening. By short-cutting any part of the sales preparation or process, they will leave gaps. Those gaps will often result in a client rejecting them and their product.

Making Assumptions—Prequalifying Your Client

Many weak salespeople make judgments about a prospective client's situation. The biggest assumption is financial. Salespeople often make financial assessments based on their impressions, including a client's clothing, gender, or a company's size or capability to afford a service.

With these biased assumptions, the weak salesperson often makes a weak presentation and lowered product recommendation that is less than what the potential client wants, needs, and would be willing to purchase if the salesperson had not attempted to make a premature decision for them.

Despite what many untrained salespeople think, price is not the only reason why people buy what they buy. Weak salespeople are often shocked that they lose a sale—not due to a lower price from another company but because another salesperson took more time to understand what the potential client wanted. Thus, allowing the client to make his or her own decisions.

Leaving Someone Out—Involve All Parties

Tom continued, "Great salespeople include everyone in the process and are highly respectful to anyone surrounding the believed decision-maker. I figured this out years ago. I had mistakenly concluded that the decision-maker was one person when it was actually the person I considered the assistant. Over the years, I've made special efforts to be genuinely respectful and courteous to everyone around, including other staff and even children who happen to be present on my sales encounters. You never know what influences the person who answers the phone, brings the coffee, sweeps the floor, or interrupts your presentation is to the decision-maker. Sometimes it's the same person!"

Steve wrote:

"Include all parties."

Using Clichés

Throughout history, stories have been an incredibly valuable way to unite, motivate, and inspire people. Top salespeople use the power of stories and analogies but avoid the use of clichés. Annoying clichés include, "You know, you get what you pay for" or "Quality doesn't come cheap."

The best kind of story is one that comes from the client's mouth—not yours. Rather than tell the client one of your stories, ask the client whether she has ever purchased anything that was more expensive than another product; then ask whether she was pleased with the outcome.

Ask your client whether she ever purchased something "cheaper" that she hoped was just as good as a more expensive brand and ended up being disappointed with the results. You will be thrilled with the stories your customers will share with you. When you create an analogy that your client understands, it makes them feel smarter. This strategy will help them see why it is important to purchase what is right, not necessarily what they originally thought they should spend.

Steve wrote:

"Get clients to reflect on a past purchase that could help this sale."

Creating Your Own Objections

Tom continued, "During the presentation stage of the sale, many salespeople create their own objections without realizing it. Although most questions are great, there are a few questions or suggestions that will get you into trouble. For example, if you ask a client if he has checked with an outside or unavailable person, you are giving your prospective client a reason to not purchase without first going and checking with that source.

Salespeople should be very proud of and confident about their product—even how their product or company compares to others. Many statements can give the client an 'out,' however. The statement, 'When you compare our product to others on the market—you will find ours is superior' is inviting—even encouraging a potential client to shop around.

Other inadvertent delaying tactics include suggesting that your client check out your company with an outside, credible source such as an industry expert or reference guide. Don't allow that. If your company has a reputation with an outside, credible source, bring the quote, article, or rating information with you.

At the end of your presentation, rather than just plowing into money issues, ask your client how he or she liked what they heard. If he or she answers positively, they will often ask you how much the item(s) are. Then, you are providing them the investment based on their request. If they happen to respond negatively, you would question them further to figure out why and address those questions or concerns before you waste your time telling a customer how much something they don't want yet, costs. This scenario is one example of objection prevention, which is the next critical element of a strong sales cycle."

Lesson 17—Objection Prevention

"Great salespeople are proactive; weak salespeople tend to be reactive," Mrs. Sellmore began. Salespeople should concentrate on objection prevention. To reach this goal, you need to know the most common objections or concerns that your clients might have. Once you determine your typical clients' most common concerns, proactively include their resolutions in your presentation.

For example, if you were selling waterbeds, a common concern of a client might be the potential of water leaking. Knowing this concern, great salespeople proactively include information in their presentation to put their potential client at ease. For example, you might say, "Some people wonder if they need to be concerned about leaking.

(Look for agreement.) Our mattresses are made with only the highest-grade vinyl and heat seals. In addition, we include a top-quality liner that could hold all of the water from the mattress so even if the mattress were to leak, water will not end up on the floor."

"Do you remember verbal affirmation?" Tom asked.

"I think so," Steve responded. "What a customer states becomes more real, and he or she becomes more 'married' to the thought. A desire that a customer states becomes more desired."

"Exactly. And, when a customer voices a concern about something, it becomes more real as well. Therefore, it's best to have done your homework to include the positive outcome of concerns during your presentation."

Steve wrote in his journal:

> "Address predictable concerns before they grow up and become objections."

Tom asked Steve if he recalled the information on body language from training.

"I do." Steve replied.

"Great," Tom continued. "Objections can occur at any time and are often openly expressed by the client but sometimes are only revealed through body language. Remember, strong salespeople read what a potential client's body is saying and figures out what they might be thinking, then addresses the issue and/or readjusts the presentation appropriately."

"For example," Tom said, "if a potential client suddenly rubs her neck while you are in the middle of your presentation, think back and ask yourself what you might have said that disturbed her. Then, try to ease her concern."

Steve wrote down:

"Watch customer's body language to detect any unspoken concerns."

Lesson 18—
Commandments of
Closing

Closing is one of the most feared parts of selling. That's usually because the close is where you ask someone to part with their money. Asking for money from someone is uncomfortable for many people. This is also where most salespeople feel they'll be rejected so they tend to approach this step with trepidation. With a little courage and practice, almost any salesperson can become a great closer. How do you become comfortable? Role-playing is a proven way to overcome fear. It helps you desensitize yourself to the fears you have.

When a doctor asks you if you want to have your medicine in chewable or tablet form—that's an alternative close. The doctor is assuming that you want the solution to your ailment and is simply offering you two alternatives. Salespeople will be successful using this technique, as well.

"The alternative close is one of my favorites because it shows complete confidence that you expect the customer to move forward with the solution, and you are just clarifying which choice," Tom continued.

When you use the alternative closing method, make sure you actually state the two choices. Back to the doctor example: asking, "Would you like the tablet form?" would assume that the patient could read the doctor's mind about the alternative chewable or liquid form. To the patient, it could actually sound like, "Do you want the tablet—or nothing?"

One of the most important things to remember when closing is patience after you ask a closing question—to be quiet and wait for the customer to respond. Too many salespeople are so nervous they just keep on talking and end up talking themselves right out of a sale. Although 15 seconds of silence might feel like 15 minutes of eternity, wait for your potential client to respond. Often, he has just a few points to clarify in his own mind on his path to becoming a new client.

"Identifying when the client is interested in moving ahead often makes the process of asking for the business much easier," Tom continued. "So when do you ask for the business? When you see a buying signal."

"What's a buying signal?" Steve asked.

Buying Signals

A buying signal is a verbal or physical indicator that the customer is interested in your product and might be ready to purchase. To be an actual buying signal, the client needs to have some understanding of what the product is or does and how much it costs.

Here are some specific buying signals that customers offer:

1. Asking about delivery time/availability

2. Taking mental or physical possession of your product or service

3. Asking anything about payment, including deposit, financing, or a discount

4. Asking permission either verbally or non-verbally from another source (counterpart, spouse, friend, you...)

Steve wrote:

"Great salespeople look for buying signals."

Why Most Salespeople Are Weak Closers

Tom continued, "Unfortunately, most salespeople receive countless buying signals without understanding their meaning. Other salespeople understand them but fail to respond effectively.

"For example, most salespeople, when asked about delivery time or inventory, would answer the question by saying, 'This unit will take four weeks to come in' and then stop talking.

"Great salespeople understand that the reason the customer is asking the question is because the customer is interested in purchasing the product. The great salesperson then assumes the sale and asks for clarification. The salesperson says, 'We can have this unit in as little as four weeks; did you decide on the blue or the red?' Or, they might say, 'what time frame best suits your schedule?' If the potential client needs to meet a specific delivery date and you know its impossible, you'll have to help them see enough value in your product to wait longer for it. If your delivery time is shorter than they require, move on to your paperwork with the delivery date they have requested."

Great Closing Questions

"Like you, when a great salesperson hears or sees a buying signal, he assumes that the client is willing to move ahead," Tom said.

"Answering the question asked, and without too much of a pause, the salesperson then asks a closing question.
How about, 'How soon would you like this delivered?' Is that a good question?" Steve asked.

Tom smiled. "That's a great question.

"If the customer wants the product, why doesn't he just ask for it?" Steve asked, puzzled.

"Customers generally don't jump up and say, 'OK, I'll take it.' They don't want to appear vulnerable, naïve, or pay too much so they naturally hesitate when it comes down to the final decision."

Top salespeople have a prepared list of closing questions with which he or she is extremely comfortable:

1. Which (one, color, model) did you decide on?

2. How soon did you want it delivered?

3. When would you like delivery?

4. How soon would you like your product or service installed—as soon as possible?

"So, you asked for the sale. Our job is over, right?" Tom asked. "For most salespeople, the job would be over. Great salespeople aren't done yet, though."

Lesson 19—Overcoming Final Objections

Sometimes your customer will state an objection after you have asked for, or assumed, the sale. Most of the time when a customer states an objection at this point, he or she is simply looking for clarification. When this situation happens, although you might want to, be careful not to overreact, appear defensive, or stop selling.

By interviewing and watching top salespeople within your own company, you will be able to prepare a list of common objections. Once that list is complete, prepare, test, and master prepared ways to effectively overcome them.

What Do You Hear When a Customer States an Objection?

Based on excellent training and diligent practice, a great salesperson hears an objection from a customer as, "Could you explain this to me better?" In contrast, the average or weak salesperson hears that same objection from the customer as, "I'm not going to buy what you're selling."

What Do You Feel When a Customer States an Objection?

To a strong, proven salesperson, an objection is as welcomed as a rain shower on a hot day because it proves that the client is interested. People won't invest their energy objecting to something in which they have no interest. So, top salespeople look at the positive side of the situation. We realize that once the client's question is satisfactorily answered in a positive manner, the salesperson can ask for or assume the sale and will usually get it.

Weak salespeople, however, view the same objection as the beginning of a hurricane that they fear and would like to avoid. This fear is eliminated and success is achieved by listing and mastering your most common objections.

Baseball players adjust their swing depending on the pitch and speed of the ball. Surgeons are trained how to respond when complications emerge. These adjustments are important in many professions, including sales.

Steve wrote:

"Don't be afraid of objections — be prepared to address them."

"I realize that it is my job to try to prevent an objection by raising and answering them myself, as you told me earlier. But what do I do if a client states another objection?" asked Steve.

Change Your Customer's Mind—Gently

Most salespeople give adequate presentations; many are even good. Countless salespeople are afraid to overcome a client's objection, however, because they are afraid of being perceived as pushy.

As we discussed before, there are many times a salesperson will want and need to help clients see a situation from a different perspective (when they don't want to move forward that day, don't want to spend as much as your product is worth, or when they want to shop around).

It is important that you present the information in such a way that your client can accept it easily, without feeling embarrassed, and believing that he's not different from others in the same situation.

A few guidelines to remember: Watch your body language and make sure that it is as open and welcoming as possible. Although you are tempted, don't cross your arms, legs, or lean back if you are sitting. Your facial expressions can be interested and even a bit surprised, but not annoyed. This all becomes easier with practice and paying attention to yourself.

Watch your words. Don't start a sentence with the word, "Well..." Well too strongly separates your position from your customers. One effective way of dealing with a customer's objection is to begin with, "That's a great question." Continue with, "Other moms/homeowners, CEOs/husbands/CEOs/managers ... whatever group the customer is or wants to be a part of ... were also interested in why this was done this way." If you can, quote an objective, independent source (a consumer reporting company, a huge company that uses and loves your product, and so on) that says your way is the best way or your product solves the challenge so that your client can more readily accept your reasoning.

This way, the client learns why your product or service is beneficial and more importantly is able to accept it, because he or she isn't alone in this thought; there are others who feel the same way.

"Here are a few advanced ways to help your customer see a different perspective," Tom said.

Feel, Felt, Found Technique

The Feel, Felt, Found strategy is an age-tested, proven strategy of moving your customers gently to a new way of thinking. There are three separate parts to Feel, Felt, Found:

1. I understand how you feel.

   This wording lets a customer know that you heard him or her and can relate.

2. Initially, other (top purchasing agents, CEOs, mothers...) felt that way.

   You are letting him or her know that this initial thought is common (meaning that the situation can change).

3. What they found, however, was that after doing 'X' was 'Y.'

'X' is what you want your customer to do (purchase your product or put a deposit down now...).

'Y' is something positive your customer will receive that he or she cares a great deal about.

This other group of people changed its minds, did what you, the salesperson, recommended they do, and were very pleased with the outcome.

"So, Steve ... tell me something you would like right now," Tom said.

Without any hesitation, Steve responded, "I want to be as successful as you, Tom."

"Steve, I understand how you feel. Initially, other ambitious salespeople felt the same way. What they discovered by staying positive and working hard at their craft each day was that they were very pleased with their own success."

Recall Strategy

The recall strategy is using the customer's words, phrases, or position to help the customer move ahead.

For example, if you are selling a piece of jewelry and, after an excellent presentation your customer says, "It's lovely, but it's so expensive," the recall strategy might be helpful. By responding respectfully, you can say, "Mary, remember when you mentioned earlier that quality was very important to you? Is this the type of quality you're referring to?"

If she answers "Yes," it will make it easier for her to isolate that this piece is the one she is looking for. Now, the two of you can figure out how she can pay for it.

If she answers "No," you can find her something with which she is more comfortable.

Reduce to the Ridiculous

So, let's say that you and your customer have determined that the product or service you are promoting is a great choice for him. The only glitch seems to be the cost.

A technique called Reducing to the Ridiculous is very effective at helping the customer see the investment differently.

Imagine that you are selling a $30,000 item. $30,000 is a lot of money in any economy. Try reducing $30,000 over the period of time your customer will be using it, which is a technique that the automobile industry is very good at mastering. Its success is obvious by the number of cars on the roads today.

Let's say that you realize that your customer is comfortable with spending only $25,000 for a new vehicle. How do you discover that? Often, a customer will volunteer the comfortable amount. If not, simply ask, "Mary, how much had you hoped to invest in a new van? Or, how much too much do you feel it is?"

Now, you take the difference between the amount of your product or service and subtract the amount that the customer is comfortable. In this case, the difference is $5,000. It would be helpful to know how long the customer plans to own or use the product or service. Then, divide the difference ($5,000) by the amount of time or number of users, when applicable.

Rather than tell the client how long you think he or she will own the product or how many users will benefit from the product, make it a question. The customer might do the math for you, but if not, you do the math for him or her. It's wise to have a calculator handy when you use this close. Let the potential client do the math themselves so it's more real to him or her than you just stating the amounts.

Ridiculous is included in the name of this close because you can reduce the amount down to one that's ridiculously low (per week, day, or even hour). For example, that $5,000 amount broken down over a five-year period is $1,000 per year (still a big number). That breaks down to only $83.33 per month, however, $19.23 per week, $2.74 per day, or just $.17 per hour (based on a sixteen-hour day). Any of those latter amounts are much more palatable than $5,000 for the average customer.

"So, for only $2.74 per day, their new car will have air conditioning, cruise control, and a better warranty?" Steve asked.

"Exactly!" Tom exclaimed.

Steve said, "What if it's a business purchase and won't be used all day every day?"

Tom replied, "You do the math based on the usage. If the business is only open five days a week, use that figure rather than seven days. If they're open eight hours a day, use that as well. The important thing is that you practice the math so you have it right when the time comes. This is such a powerful close, it's worth investing your time in figuring out several scenarios."

Steve wrote down:

> "Reduce the purchase price or the difference down to a day."

"Which technique should I use with most customers?" Steve asked.

"Top salespeople often use numerous techniques to help each customer see that it is in his or her best interest to move ahead immediately—that it's worth more to them to have the product or service than it is to keep their money," Tom said.

"Genuine concern for your client, combined with professionalism and numerous strategies, will help him or her see your persistence as concern rather than pushiness."

Lesson 20—Facts and Fears of Follow-Up

"Steve, there are two groups of people who deserve or require follow-up: prospective clients who have not yet purchased from you and clients who have already purchased from you," Tom said.

"If you didn't get the order while you were with your prospective client, you can increase the chances for recovery with excellent follow-up skills. Most salespeople are reluctant to call a prospective client back. They might feel as if they are bothering the person or, they reason, if the client were interested, he or she would call them back."

If you have connected with your clients during your time with them and exemplified the traits of a professional, they will not be put off; rather, they will usually be impressed. This method provides another strategic and powerful edge over the competition.

Following up with a client demonstrates a strong work ethic. It shows the clients that they are more than a number and that you remembered them and their needs. Contrary to what most salespeople believe, calling back often gives clients a sense of comfort. They assume that you will be there for them after the sale.

Follow-up demonstrates that you are the type of person who is not only willing but also eager to provide more than what is expected.

"What is the best method for following up? Mail, fax, e-mail, or phone?" Steve asked.

"Generally, by phone," Tom said. "It's fast and provides a two-way dialogue."

While you are with a client, make sure that you get the direct and alternative numbers as well as the best time to be reached.

"When should I follow up?" Steve asked.

"When you've *told* him or her that you are going to," Tom replied. "Most salespeople make the mistake of *asking* their prospective client when they would like a follow-up call. This gives up friendly control and often results in the client putting off the decision indefinitely."

Top salespeople tell the client that they will call him or her on X day (in the morning or afternoon) to answer any additional questions or to begin the delivery process. If the client does not object, assume you have received their permission.

Remember, your client's sense of focus, urgency, and interest is generally piqued during the presentation. The sooner the follow-up, the better (generally within 24 to 48 hours after your meeting).

"What should I say?" Steve asked.

"What you shouldn't say is anything like 'I was calling to see if you decided to buy my product or not.' It's better to begin by telling the customer positive things about the product that you may have forgotten to mention during your time together. Or, give them a brief summary of all the things they said they liked about your product or service. Then, offer an alternative choice such as 'Did you decide on the (blue or the red)?'"

How Often Do You Follow Up?

"You follow up until you obtain the sale," Tom said. "I often call clients back that other salespeople have given up on. I usually get a few sales a month just from following up."

Thank-You Notes

Another competitive advantage is sending a handwritten, personalized note to your client.

"So I should send a thank-you note to each client who buys?" Steve asked.

"Yes, and ideally everyone who didn't buy." Tom replied. Here is an example:

> Dear Bob:
> It was great meeting with you. I am confident that you are going to enjoy your gorgeous new (office furniture). I look forward to serving the needs of both you and your company and will follow up with you shortly.
> Respectfully,
> Tom

If you worked in some retail situations, it might be difficult to send a handwritten thank-you note to each client you spoke with, but you certainly could send one to each client with which you spent more time.

Following up with the client who did buy from you will be a tremendous benefit to you in many ways. First, there is no better source of motivation for a salesperson who hears directly from a real, live client how great the product is. That information is priceless! It can and should be incorporated into future presentations. That is third-party confirmation—more credible than your accounts alone. Second, you are helping these people reduce buyer's remorse—a very normal and preventable part of a purchase. Additionally, once these people give your product or service the accolades that it deserves, it's a perfect time to ask for referrals. Top salespeople multiply their sales by this strategy alone.

During follow up, you will want to be mentally prepared for a new client to have a case of buyer's remorse. Buyer's remorse is a predictable and normal part of the sales process—especially when the customer spent more than they initially thought they would. Buyer's remorse is when a customer begins doubting the usefulness, necessity, or cost of their purchase.

Great salespeople work to proactively reduce buyer's remorse by implementing the following strategies:

1. Doing a great presentation that is highly involved and therefore, highly memorable, will create longer happier memories that help diminish buyer's remorse.

2. The Socratic method of dialog helps reduce buyer's remorse because the customer is articulating his or her preferences, which your product or service answers.

3. Congratulating, assuring, and restating the value that other customers have received from similar purchases also helps reduce buyer's remorse.

Follow up is a key element in keeping sales closed and in building your business through referrals.

Lesson 21—The Competitive Advantage of Referrals

"Steve, when I first started in sales with this company, our product was unknown. We didn't have much money for advertising. It was critical to our company and me personally that as many prospects as possible heard about us. We hoped that people would tell their friends and associates about it, and asked each new client to provide our company with at least one referral."

I have many clients who have provided me with numerous solicited and unsolicited referrals, because they know I provide exceptional service and will help them with anything I can.

When you dazzle your clients, you are prompting the most powerful advertising of all: word-of-mouth referrals. This type of promotion is far more economical and much more profitable than investing in the largest billboards, the cleverest jingles, or even a full-page ad."

"Don't take any client for granted, and don't wait for another client to walk through the door," Tom advised. "Don't wait for the company to mandate the implementation of a referral program. Ask for referrals with every sales opportunity, including the clients who decided not to buy from you."

"Wait a minute," said Steve, "you want me to ask someone for a referral when they didn't buy the product themselves?"

"Absolutely," replied Tom. "Don't assume they didn't buy because there's something wrong with the product. It may just not be right for them. That doesn't mean they don't know someone else for whom the product might be just the thing they're looking for. If you've been professional and demonstrated that you give sincere service, the non-client shouldn't feel uncomfortable at all about giving you the name of someone else you might serve.

It is much easier to successfully promote your product or service to a referral. That referral already has the testimonial of a respected friend or colleague. Referrals also have far fewer objections, including the need to shop around, because they know that the referral source is pleased with you or the source wouldn't have referred them to you."

Steve wrote down:

"Referrals make the best leads."

Tom asked Steve how he would ask for a referral after making a sale. Steve said, "Well, Mr. Johnson, now that you've recognized the benefits of our fine product by taking ownership, are there any other people who come to mind who might benefit from it?"

"Not bad for a first effort," said Tom. "However, it's way too easy for Mr. Johnson to say no. You've given him the whole world to think about. It's much more effective to continue to draw from something the client said during your conversations. For example, when establishing rapport, if the client mentions something about another division of the company, you'll want to specifically ask whom you should talk with in that division about their needs for our product."

Here are some basic steps for getting quality referrals:

1. Isolate faces for them to see by referring to something they said.

2. Use 3 x 5 cards to write down the names provided.

3. Ask qualifying questions about the people named.

4. Ask for addresses and phone numbers for the names provided.

5. Ask the referrer to call and introduce you.

6. If they are uncomfortable making the introduction, ask permission to use their name when you call these people.

7. Say, "I promise to do my best to give them the same excellent service I've given you."

That last point is critical. You are not just begging for names but sincerely want to serve someone else this person might know. If you do a good job, you'll be making the referrer look good in the eyes of the new referral.

Most salespeople could increase their business by 10%, 20%, 50% or even double their business with little effort by obtaining referrals with each sales appointment. Most salespeople don't because they let fear stop them. If you work past the fear of this and other uncomfortable parts of this training, you will be thrilled with the results.

Lesson 22—The Vision of a Great Salesperson: Goals

"During training, you heard goals mentioned quite a bit, didn't you?" Mrs. Sellmore asked.

"I did," Steve replied. "I found that interesting."

"Interesting is good, but let's figure out your particular goals," she continued. "The human mind is like a missile. When you give your mind a target, your brain—combined with your hard work—finds a way to hit it. Most people do not set a target for themselves, so their brain subconsciously wastes energy searching for a target and sadly falls short of its immense potential."

If you want to be a top sales professional or own a highly successful and profitable business—or achieve anything exceptional—you must learn to set goals. Goals are a charting device. They let you know where you are going and how you are doing. Poorly defined goals, however, will not result in success. The power of defining and visualizing your goals is in direct proportion to actually achieving them. Writing down those goals helps you remember and clarify them in your mind.

It doesn't make any sense for us to go any further until you have your goals clarified and written down. Take as much time as you need to write down your professional sales goals, your personal goals, and a financial goal. Ask yourself, "What lifestyle do I want in 20 years? Where will I have to be in 10 years to achieve that 20-year goal?" Cut your 10-year goals in half. Keep breaking your goals down until you know what you must do today to work toward that lifestyle you dream about in 20 years.

"I'll definitely put some time into my goals later," Steve said.

Tom firmly interjected, "It doesn't make any sense for us to work on making you successful if we don't know what 'success' means to you. Let's go over the elements of a true goal."

Great Salespeople are Great Goal Setters

A true goal is:

- Written down, highly visible, and referred to often

- Quantifiable or measurable in time, dates, and amounts

- Realistic yet challenging

- Most importantly, something you have to really want

So, Steve went off to a quiet place and thought about what he wanted. He had a difficult time with this exercise. He wanted to sell as much as possible. Wasn't that enough of a goal? Knowing that he needed to be more specific, Steve continued to work through the process, and he finally figured out his sales, personal, and financial goals. After he finished this exercise, he met with Tom and Mrs. Sellmore again.

"How did you do with your goals?" asked Tom.

"OK, I think," he replied.

"Let's see," he said. "I see you really put thought into this. These look great!"

"I know you aren't telling me that just because I wrote these goals down on paper, that I'm going to achieve them—are you?" Steve asked.

"No, these are outcome goals—what you want to end up with," he replied. "They need to be viewed daily and combined with an activity plan and a lot of work."

Activity Plan

An activity plan defines what activities and tasks you must complete to achieve your outcome goals. For example, how many customers will you have to find or talk to, based on your existing conversion ratio and closing ratio, to reach your monthly sales goal?

Calculating Your Conversion Ratio

"What's a conversion ratio?" Steve asked.

"Your conversion ratio is the number of people you or your office has to speak with to get one opportunity to see a prospective client to present your product or service," Tom replied. "Most salespeople and businesses overlook this gold mine and just wait for another client to come to them. Many salespeople and businesses can substantially increase their sales by paying attention to the conversion process and by making improvements in their script and other techniques.

When we first started tracking this in our company, we discovered that when 10 people called in for information, our receptionist could convert only five of those calls to appointments. We discovered that the reason was because she was trying to be too helpful, giving out too much information on the original phone call. The company provided her additional training, and now she converts 10 calls into eight appointments. That means that we have 30 percent greater return on the same advertising budget and 30 percent more potential clients to speak with in-person."

Calculating Your Closing Ratio

"Your closing ratio is how many people you speak with or meet with compared to how many people actually buy from you," he said. "So, out of that first eight, we can calculate how many people actually purchased from us."

Once you have these numbers, you can determine how many clients you need to speak to, based on your closing ratio, to end up with as many sales as you need to meet your monthly goal. Here is a formula sheet so you can have it when you are ready to sell.

1. Conversion ratio = phone calls ÷ number of appointments (10 phone calls ÷ 8 appointments = 80% conversion ratio)

2. Closing ratio = presentations ÷ number of sales (10 presentations ÷ 5 closed sales = 50% closing ratio)

Calculating the Number of Needed Sales

Tom continued, "We need to know what our average sale and current closing ratio is to properly assess how many potential customers we have to contact. For simplicity's sake, let's say that I have a $10,000 average sale. If my closing rate were 50 percent, then I would need to find 20 potential customers to reach a $100,000 goal. Be careful not to count on 10 closings, because you will undoubtedly have postponements or cancellations. So, I count on the number I need *plus* 10 percent—in this case, 11. Always overshoot your goal. It is far more rewarding to say that you sold *more than* $100,000 rather than *almost* $100,000.

"I now know that I need 11 clients a month at an average sale of $10,000 to hit my goal. This is much easier to understand than just saying I need $110,000 in sales," Tom said.

"Divide the number of sales by the number of working days in the month, and you know your daily goal," Tom advised Steve. "Then, go to your sales journal (as well as notes on your bathroom mirror, dashboard, and so on) and write down your daily goals. If I ever fall short of obtaining my daily goal, I roll over the deficit to the next day's goal. If it is a huge number, I spread the deficit evenly over my daily activities for the month."

"What's the point of tracking them? Shouldn't you just work as hard as you can to get them as high as possible?" Steve asked.

"Great salespeople do both. We develop an activity plan that is our daily blueprint of what we need to do to achieve our goals, and we work hard at doing what it takes to achieve them," he replied.

Steve wrote:

> "First — goals; then figure out how to get there — activity plan"

"Steve," Tom continued, "we've had a full, busy day. It's been fun working with you. You have great potential. Go home, relax, review your notes and the techniques in your journal, and we will see you and the rest of the new employees in Mrs. Sellmore's training center tomorrow morning at 8 A.M. sharp."

Steve thanked Tom and drove home—his mind spinning with ideas.

The next morning, Steve was groomed and dressed sharply, wide-awake, and energized by his two-mile run and healthy breakfast. He arrived early in the training room.

Soon, other attendees arrived. Wendy walked in and noticed Steve. She sat down next to him and whined, "More training, huh? This is a lot of work. I sure hope it pays off." Steve didn't see Jack anywhere and wondered if he was running late again.

Just then, Mrs. Sellmore entered and welcomed back the new employees." This morning, we will finish the classroom portion of your training. Then, each of you will go on an actual sales call with your coaches."

Steve listened carefully, because he was thrilled to hear that Tom would be taking him to an actual sales call.

Lesson 23—Time Planning

"Each one of you already has something in common with our top performers—and our less-than top performers," Mrs. Sellmore began.

"Our top performers also have something interesting in common with weaker performers," she said. The group looked puzzled. "Along with you, each group of salespeople has exactly 86,400 seconds per day and 1,400 minutes per day. The top performers, however, use their time very differently than the less successful salespeople. Our objective during this training is to provide you with the most powerful techniques to maximize your productivity. Our top salespeople guard their time jealously and plan out their professional days to achieve their goals."

The benefits of planning your time include the following:

1. Increased productivity

2. Increased job satisfaction

3. Improved interpersonal relationships

"Since you will all be on the go, we recommend that you find a portable control device," Mrs. Sellmore advised. "Salespeople by nature are generally very optimistic people. We often think we can accomplish more than is sometimes realistic. Over-committing can get you into a lot of trouble, including spending valuable time in less-than-productive tasks. A personal data assistant will help you monitor and organize your time and activities. Two options are electronic versions or paper planners.

Always carry your planning tool with you and make sure it has a phone directory so you can make your phone calls from anywhere. Good planners will have a month-at-a-glance area, in addition to daily activity sections, that allow you to list and prioritize each task.

Using your time wisely will not only increase your productivity, but it will also help prevent future problems such as not returning calls when you need to. It also eliminates guilt, because you will know that you are spending time on the right activity. It will help you stay balanced by ensuring that you spend the appropriate quality and quantity of time with your loved ones, as well."

"A specific barrier that will block your path to success is procrastination," she continued. "Tom, would you let the group know what specific strategies you use to minimize procrastination, please?"

"I'd be happy to," Tom replied. "First of all, I enter everything—each task that I want to accomplish into my PDA. Then, I prioritize the list and do the most important things first. If doing the task immediately isn't possible, I schedule time to do it."

"That seems pretty time consuming in itself," Wendy commented.

"Actually, it really isn't once you create good habits," Tom responded. "I enter everything as it comes up so it's just a part of the process of my day. I found that this system not only is quick and straightforward, but it saves me a great deal of time by not making costly mistakes like forgetting something important to a client or family member.

In addition, every night I have a five to ten minute meeting with myself before bedtime. I sit down with my time planner and quickly relive my day. Then, I determine the six most important things I must do the next day. This helps me sleep like a baby. Each morning I have a 15-minute review to get me focused on what I am going to accomplish."

Be careful to avoid time wasters, including having a disorganized desk. Clean your desk off every day. It will help you be more productive the next day when you come into the office and see a clean desk. Try to not hang on to paper too long (file it or toss it). This activity will help you avoid looking at messy piles of paper and save you the time of going through them time and again.

The same guidelines apply to your car. The neater and more organized it is, the easier it will be for you to maximize your productivity while in it.

No one will care more about your success than you, and therefore you need to learn to guard your time jealously. As you become more and more successful, you will have more and more demands on your time. Although we encourage you to be generous of your time with others, there will be times when you will need to say no to others. We are not referring to customers, of course. We are speaking about possibly coworkers. Always be polite and gracious. Tell the person what you *can do* or when you can fulfill a request rather than taking on their task immediately. This action will sometimes help reduce their disappointment and help them understand how busy you are.

Remember, spend 75 percent of your time prospecting until you have enough clients to provide you with the income you have set as your goal and 15 percent prospecting when you think you have enough.

Lesson 24—Self-Analysis of Great Salespeople

"We are confident that each of you will have your share of successes," Mrs. Sellmore said. "Unfortunately, you will also have your share of setbacks and not get every sale. This is part of sales."

Mrs. Sellmore continued, "When a great baseball player strikes out, he often asks his coach or teammates, 'What did he get me out with?' Then, he works hard at not missing in the same situation again.

When weak salespeople lose a sale, they blame the client, a competitor, the economy, or some other outside source and then passively wait for the next client to come their way.

When a great salesperson loses a sale, however, he or she thinks just like a top athlete—asking what could have been done differently."

"Remember, great salespeople tend to see the glass as half full," she said. "Great salespeople ground themselves by objectively and accurately measuring many things, including their conversion ratios, closing ratios, and average sale as your coaches have discussed with you. The charting of sales performance helps determine how they are doing in comparison to their goals and to other salespeople."

Sales Journal/Tracking System

Unlike baseball players, salespeople generally don't often have coaches standing by when they do their closing or overtly monitoring each sales transaction.

A tracking system forces us to take a clear look at our performance and progress. Athletes in training, for example, use a journal system to track their performances, their training regimens, and results.

Many salespeople are not very analytical or organized. A great salesperson pushes past such analytical and organizational deficiencies and uses a system that tracks the following things:

- Daily goal

- The necessary daily activity (not results) to correspond to the monthly or quarterly goal

- Number of calls made

- Number of customers met with

- Follow-up information on each prospect

- If no sale was made, why not? What was the stated objection?

- Action needed to get the sale and what could have been done differently to keep this situation from happening again

- List of customers for follow-up, including asking for referrals

- Daily, weekly, and monthly closing ratio

- Daily, weekly, and monthly average sale

- List of sales lost, to which companies, and why (include changes to prevent this from happening again, if possible, adding them to the sales presentation guide)

"I'm going to need a secretary to track all of this!" Jack blurted out.

Wondering who hired Jack, Mrs. Sellmore explained, "The process of writing down your performance details heightens your awareness of performance and helps you decide whether your current level is acceptable. It shouldn't take more than a few minutes at the end of each day yet provides extremely valuable feedback.

Once you have determined what your weaknesses are, you are well on your way to improving them. Role-playing with a manager or fellow employee or videotaping and/or audiotaping your presentation will give you a more accurate look and 'listen' on how you are doing and what you need to improve.

Recently, I was asked to help train four salespeople whose sales were down. I asked them which objection they most often received from their customers. They thought they knew their most common objections, but didn't have documentation to back them up. I asked them to keep a sales journal for one month and report their progress.

One month later, the group reported a 23 percent increase in closing ratio and a 13 percent increase in average sale. We are convinced that the combination of training and the tracking of the sales journal were the keys to that improvement. Forcing them to look at their performance was a catalyst for change. They became serious very quickly about improving. They implemented the many tools they were given during their training. Those techniques, by the way, are the same techniques your coaches and I have given each of you. I strongly recommend that you review the content and begin implementing what we've covered in training for at least 20–30 minutes each day as you begin your own selling career with our company."

With that, Mrs. Sellmore wished all the employees her best, letting them know that her door was always open to each of them.

The coaches entered and greeted each of their assigned salespeople.

"Are you ready to watch your first appointment?" Tom asked Steve.

"You bet!" Steve exclaimed.

The Appointment

After they returned to the office, Steve said, "Wow! Are all sales that easy? You did everything you taught me. Even I was excited by the presentation, and I knew what you were going to say. She really liked you and our product. I'm sure she's going to be pleased with her purchase."

"I'm confident she will be, but I'll follow up just to make sure. Now that you've finished your training, you need to go out on your own, practice, practice, practice, and apply what you've learned to your own career. Steve, I really think you have what it takes to become a Certified Salesperson."

"How do I do that?" Steve asked.

"You attend a special training seminar, study, and then take a test. If you pass, you will become a CGSP™—Certified Graduate Salesperson—a distinction reserved for salespeople who are truly serious about doing well in their careers."

Steve went out, worked diligently, and applied all that he had learned. Each day he set aside a minimum of an hour to read, study, and keep his journal. At times, the hours were longer than he initially thought but he found it all interesting and helpful.

During his initial practice sessions, he was very nervous and struggled. But after a few weeks, he felt more confident and he saw his numbers rise significantly.

Later that month, Jack called to see whether Steve wanted to meet him and Wendy for lunch. Steve was eager to hear about Jack and Wendy's progress and to tell them about his successes.

The Lunch

Steve had closed one of his biggest sales to date just before he arrived at the restaurant. Energetically, Steve greeted Jack, who was already seated at a table waiting for him. Steve was surprised to see Jack drinking a beer. Steve decided not to say anything.

Wendy came in late. She seemed rushed and frazzled. When they all finally relaxed, they began discussing their experiences since training.

"So, how do you like sales?" Wendy asked Steve.

"I really like it. When I decided to take this sales job, I wasn't sure I'd stay with it. But I committed to give it my all and found the analytical and psychological processes fascinating. I, in some way do feel like a doctor who is helping his patients, and I'm making more money than I ever expected. I love sales! I'm hooked!" he said.

"You've got to be kidding," Jack exclaimed. "This is only a job!"

"No, seriously, it's amazing to see how the sales process really is like a chess game," Steve said. "I try to use all the techniques we were given during our training, along with the tips my coach provided me. How are you doing, Wendy?"

"I'm doing all right, I guess, but I think I have the worst area," she said. "It's really hard work, and my customers aren't interested in paying for this product."

Steve empathized with Wendy and tried to remind her of some of the techniques that they had learned during training.

"When a sale doesn't go well," he suggested, "I check my journal to see what I could have done differently."

"I tried that once," Wendy whined. "All that tracking is like homework. It doesn't work—at least, not in my market with the way the economy is right now."

Steve decided it was pointless to give any more suggestions. "Jack, you've had more experience than all of us put together," said Steve. "How are you doing?"

"I'm doing OK in this racket," Jack said. "I use my usual spiel that's seemed to get me by for all these years. My income's the same as before."

Jack's attention shifted to the game on television. Steve worried about his colleagues.

Months Later

Steve was filled with anticipation as he walked into his first regional sales training. Mrs. Sellmore greeted him with obvious pleasure. Steve now understood the value of such a warm greeting. He was even more determined to continue to practice all of the same principles that she had imparted.

Steve was thrilled to see Tom and couldn't wait to tell him about his progress and that he passed the test and was an actual CGSP—"Certified Graduate Salesperson.™" The meeting was about to begin, but before he had a chance to speak with Tom, he needed to take a seat. He looked around to see where Wendy and Jack were. Steve spotted Wendy toward the back of the room but didn't see Jack.

Tom caught his attention and motioned for Steve sit up front with him. He did so.

Everyone began coming into the room. The room was filled with bodies and a ton of positive energy. Upbeat music began to play. Everyone started clapping as the CEO of the company entered the room.

"Welcome to our first quarter regional meeting!" the CEO exclaimed.

After a few moments, the CEO told the group that it was time to announce the first quarter's results. The room got quiet.

"The region with the top sales this quarter is ... the Northeast division!!!" the CEO exclaimed.

The room exploded with applause.

"Let's see their numbers." The CEO clicked his pointer and brought up the company's numbers. Tom was the top salesperson again ... but Steve could not believe that he was a close second.

"Tom, would you come up and say a few words?" the CEO asked.

"Absolutely! We've had a great first quarter. I have personally had the pleasure to work with a great team and am impressed with how well many of them are doing. One of our newest salespeople, Steve, has worked very hard and you can see his incredible results."

Steve noticed that Wendy's numbers weren't very good, and he didn't see Jack's name on the screen at all.

Tom continued, "I've learned over the years that there are three types of salespeople."

Three Types of Salespeople

1. Those who take the profession of sales seriously and work hard at it. They don't let fear stop them. They love their careers, and they are highly successful.

2. Those who could do well in sales but don't. They blame outside forces and don't apply themselves as much as they could. They don't seem to like their careers and barely eke out a living but can't figure out why.

3. Those who think that selling is beneath them and don't take it seriously. These people don't last long in this career.

Steve was glad that he was among those in the first group. He works hard at sales and has a fulfilling, successful career. He continues to enjoy his career and his success. We are confident that when you implement all of these lessons, you will too.

Endnotes

1. "Guided Imagery."
    http://www.holisticonline.com/guided-imagery.htm,
    accessed October 22, 2001.

2. Ibid.

3. www.discoverfitness.com/why_exercise.html

4. http://www.gsu.edu/~wwwfit/benefits.html

5. "Vitamins/Minerals."
    http://www.holisticonline.com/vitamins/
    vit-nutr-def.htm, accessed October 22, 2001.

6. www.holisticonline.com/massage/mas_home.htm
    accessed October 22, 2001.

7. National Sleep Foundation's Sleep in America Poll
    (March 2001). http://www.steepfoundation.org/
    PressArchives/lessfun_lesssleep.html, accessed
    October 22, 2001.

8. *Keep Your Brain Alive*, Lawrence C. Katz, Ph.D.,
    Manning Rubin, and David Suter, Workman Publishing
    (1999).

9. *Silent Messages: Implicit Communication of Emotions and
    Attitudes, 2nd Ed*. Albert Mehrabian, Ph.D., Belmont, CA:
    Wadsworth Publishing Company (1981).

10. *Dress For Success*, John T. Malloy, New York: Warner
    Books (1988).

11. *The Complete Idiot's Guide™ to Philosophy* by Jay Stevenson, Alpha books, A division of Macmillan Reference USA, A Simon and Schuster Macmillan Company, 1633 Broadway, New York, NY 10019-6785

12. http://www.dictionary.com

13. *Webster's New World Dictionary*, August 1983, Warner Books, Inc., 666 Fifth Avenue, New York, NY 10103

14. Ibid.

Internet Resources:

www.DailyInBox.com
www.Uinspire.com

Index